Mary Queen of Scots trial and martyrdom.
A stage play.

David Rizzio

Published in 2023 by FeedARead.com Publishing

Copyright © David Rizzio

The author or authors assert their moral right under the Copyright, Designs and Patents Act, 1988, to be identified as the author or authors of this work.

All Rights reserved. No part of this publication may be reproduced, copied, stored in a retrieval system, or transmitted, in any form or by any means, without the prior written consent of the copyright holder, nor be otherwise circulated in any form of binding or cover other than that in which it is published and without a similar condition being imposed on the subsequent purchaser.

A CIP catalogue record for this title is available from the British Library.

```
Copyright Frank J Dougan
23/11/2022
Dedicated to my mother Isobel Russell
Brennan Dougan.
1929-2013.
```

Chapter One

Mary Queen of Scots.

My End is my Beginning

Her Trial and Execution

Characters:
Mary Queen of Scots (Mary Stuart mid-40s)
William Cecil (Baron Burghley 60s)
Sir Francis Walsingham (Queen Elizabeth's Spy-master late 50s)
Judge (mid 50s)
Queen Elizabeth (mid 50s)
Earl of Kent (mid 40s)
Earl of Shrewsbury (mid 40s)
Andrew Melville (mid 50s)
Davidson (Elizabeth's secretary mid 40s)
Captain of the guard (mid 30s)

ACT 1

Scene 1

Mary Queen of Scots was a martyr for her Catholic
faith and she should be canonized for her dedication and love of the faith she could easily have renounced to have kept her throne and life.

She was surrounded by evil but she defied the bitter hatred against her and her Roman Catholic Faith.
The trial and conviction of Mary Stuart 1542-87 was the mastermind of William Cecil (Baron Burghley) 1520-98 he was the most trusted Minister in the government of Elizabeth I of England 1533-1603.

Another major player in the plot to have Mary Stuart executed was Sir Francis Walsingham c.1530-90 he was Secretary of State of England from 1573.
The place of the trial was held at Fotheringhay Castle in Northamptonshire.

Cecil had meticulously planned the trial settings.
According to the 'Act for the Queen's Safety', Mary was to be tried by a commission of twenty-four nobles and Privy Councillors who were advised by common-law

judges, approximately 33 Councillors took part in the court proceedings .

The place chosen for the court room, a space 69ft long by 21ft wide, divided by a rail at waist height.

On the 12th October 1586 CECIL sent a delegation to the prison cell within Fotheringhay Castle in which MARY STUART was being detained informing her that she was to be put on trial.

(.....Represents a Pause.....)

(WILLIAM CECIL,Baron Burghley is in his private apartment which is very dull and gray with only a desk and few chairs. He tells the captain of the guard, very abruptly)....

CECIL
'Take these orders to the prisoner,read the order then leave the document with her,... understood'?.....

(The CAPTAIN takes the document and replies sharply).

CAPTAIN
'Yes my Lord shall I take some of my guards officers with me'?

(CECIL tells him while handing him the

document).

CECIL
.....' Yes take some men with you to witness you reading the document and handing it to her,... carry on and report back as soon as you have done this'.....

(The delegation goes to the sparse room where Mary is held);

(The CAPTAIN says)

CAPTIAN
'Excuse me madam I have been ordered to bring this to you,.... it states that you have to attend court proceedings in the Great Hall here at Fotheringay'.....

(He hands MARY the parchment demanding her to appear before the commissioners);

(MARY refuses to appear before the commission and she states with a powerful statement in her heavy French accent)
Mary
'Je suis la reine absolue... et ne rien faire qui soit de mines mai préjudice propre majesté royale princes ou d'autres dans mon palais et de grade,. ou de mon fils......
Mon esprit n'est pas encore découragé,......
ni ce que je couler sous ma calamité'.....

(The CAPTAIN replies embarrassingly
)......

CAPTAIN
'Pardon me Your Majesty I apologize profusely can you repeat as I do not speak the French language'...

(MARY in English).....

MARY
'I am an absolute Queen and will do nothing which may prejudice either mine own royal majesty,.... or other princes in my palace and rank,..or my son..My mind is not yet dejected neither will I sink under my calamity'...

(The delegation returns to Cecil with her reply).

(The CAPTAIN tells him)

CAPTAIN
...... 'She refuses to acknowledge your authority'....

(CECIL goes into a rage banging his fist on his desk).

CECIL
.....'This damned woman who does she think she is'?....

(The next day Thursday 13th of October Cecil leads a delegation to Mary's cell to arrange for her to appear before the commission.

(MARY faces CECIL staring into his eyes and tells him indignantly)....

(CECIL shouts at her with some anger)

CECIL
.....'Madam, ...we are not in France could you please speak in English'...

(MARY finding this funny retorts haughtily)...

Mary
.........' I am a Queen and not a subject..if I appeared,... I should betray the majesty of Kings,
and it would be tantamount to a confession that I am bound to submit to the laws of England,... even in matters touching religion.
I am willing to answer all questions,.... provided I am interrogated before a free Parliament, ...and not before these commissioners,...
who doubtless have been carefully chosen,and who have probably already condemned me unheard...

(She speaks with a sinister/sarcastic smile)

....'Look to your consciences and remember that the theatre of the whole world is wider than the
kingdom of England'....

(CECIL interrupts MARY and tells her adamantly) ...

CECIL
.....'the commissioners could proceed to judgment in   your absence'.
(He asks her with impudence)

.....'Will you therefore answer us or not?... If you refuse the commissioners will continue to act according to their authority'...

(MARY replies with a strong voice)

Mary
'Je suis une reine......"I am myself a Queen,... the daughter of a King,... a stranger, and the true
Kinswoman of the Queen of England....I came to
England on my cousin's promise of assistance against
my enemies and rebel subjects and was at

once imprisoned...As an absolute Queen,... I cannot submit to orders,... nor can I submit to the laws of the land without injury to myself,... the King my son and all other sovereign princes...For myself I do not recognize the laws of England.... nor do I know or understand them as I have often asserted. ...I am alone without counsel,... or anyone to speak on my behalf.... My papers and notes have been taken from me,... so that I am destitute of all aid, taken at a disadvantage."...

(Stamping her feet and turns her back to CECIL)

(CECIL retorts angrily)

CECIL
...' The Queen, my mistress, knows no other Queen in her realm but herself'.

(CECIL and the delegation leave slamming the door muttering curses.
He returns later in the afternoon.)

(He announces to MARY in a loud voice);

CECIL
...'The commissioners will proceed

tomorrow in the cause,... even if you are absent and continue in your contumacy'...

(MARY replies in a heated retort with her eyes wide holding her hand up to quieten Cecil)

MARY
'Recherche de votre conscience,... à votre honneur mai Dieu vous récompense et vous pour votre jugement contre moi'...

(CECIL turns and leave her he is in a rage)

(The next day On Friday 14th October CECIL returns with SIR FRANCIS WALSINGHAM and the committee and demand she attends the court)

(WALSINGHAM playing the nice mannered approach asking her)...

WALSINGHAM
'Please madam this is for your own benefit to hear the charges against yourself... and to defend yourself in front of the commission and judges'...

(MARY exhausted by the constant pressure reluctantly agrees to appear before the commissioners sighing heavily she sinks onto her chair at her desk)

(She speaks to them in a quiet reply

ignoring them... but not looking at anyone staring and talking to the barred window)

      MARY.
.....'Yes I will attend your court and defend my self and my faith,... however I know in my heart and soul... that I will never be given a fair hearing by you and your commission and judges.
......You have kept me captive for nigh on 20 years,... yet I have done no wrong against anyone...
......My health has been destroyed... my life has been destroyed by your evil castles and prisons... and terrible treatment because.... I am the Only Catholic Queen ...
    (Strongly and emphatic)
...'Je suis la reine catholique'...
.......My sister Elizabeth has taken vengeance upon me....
.......I have had constant lies portrayed against me....

(CECIL, WALSINGHAM and the delegation storm out of her room with CECIL stammering curses)

    MARY (Calling after them)
    I am not afraid of any of you and God will judge me... and forgive me any sin I have made,... and I ask Him to forgive you... for the torment you

have put me through and have mercy on
your souls when you meet Him'!...

(CECIL meets with WALSINGHAM in his
chambers (Who is the spy-master of
England)

(He tells him venomously)

CECIL
'In Parliament... all the members of the
Privy Councillors have called
vociferously for her execution and argued
that she is no longer a Queen. ...She
deserves no favours.
She is no Queen of ours,.. she is none of
our anointed....
The examples of the Old Testament be not
few for the putting of a wicked King to
death'...

(Waslingham quietly retorts)

WALSINGHAM
....'Yes I know this sir,... and I have
read your book.. 'The Detection', ...you
wrote it very well ,....
I intend to use your own words against her
in court,... if I have your
permission'....
...'You call her a Jezebel... and
Athalia,.. Idolatress,... a most wicked
and filthy woman you name her the monstrous

and huge Dragon... and mass of the earth...

...She has been a killer of her husband, an adulteress,... a common disturber of the peace of this realm,.... and for that you have to be dealt with as an enemy....

And therefore my advice to the court will be.... to cut off her head and make no more ado about her'...

(Cecil gloatingly replies)

CECIL
'Aye that will be excellent,... now let us go forth to carry out this destiny'.
....but I will be prosecuting the case against her and I will call on your advice during the proceedings.....
...It has taken us many years to reach this point and
now we have her within our grasp... to dispose of this wretched woman for all eternity'...

(CURTAIN)

SCENE 2

(MARY takes her place in the court she sits on a high backed wooden chair with a red velvet cushion at the end of the long table, directly facing CECIL.
WALSINGHAM is sitting at the far left of the table with other English Lords.
She is dressed in a black velvet dress with gold trimming and a small white pearl decorated skull cap.
In the room she is facing the grim faced bearded men behind a long table with many people standing around the room.
There is an empty large chair on Mary's right, risen above the table at the end with a plaque with the English coat of Arms to represent Queen Elizabeth's authority.

(MARY registers her protest saying before she sits down)

MARY
.... 'I protest my innocence' ......

(Prosecuting councillor CECIL opens the case against her he is near the end of the long table opposite Mary, the JUDGE sits at the middle of the table).

(CECIL is dressed in black he stands up and addresses the room)

CECIL

.....'My Lords and Gentlemen... we are here today to present to the court the treasonable acts of Mary Stuart ...formerly the Queen of Scotland... against our Majesty Queen Elizabeth... and the plot by Mary Stuart's accomplices to murder our Gracious Majesty'...

(Loud cries and shouts go out around the room)

BACKGROUND VOICES

......'Shame on Mary Stuart and Scotland, put her to death'.

(MARY jumps up from her seat and calls out loudly as she is standing)

MARY

'Je ne reconnais pas l'autorité de ce....tribunal... et je n'ai aucune...

...raison d'avoir été invité ici comme ...je l'ai fait pas mal aux yeux de ...mon Sauveur Jésus Christ'...

(CECIL complains to the JUDGE who is on his right-hand-side)

CECIL

.....' Your honour can you please instruct the defendant to speak in English.... as we are not in Paris'...

(The JUDGE replies austerely)

JUDGE
.......' Madam... kindly address your replies in the English language... as none of the councillors here are versed in the French tongue'...

(He holds his handkerchief to his mouth and coughs gently)

(MARY replies with a rye smile and a curtsy)...
MARY
......'Certainement votre honneur'
.....'I do not recognize the authority of this court... and I have no reason to have been called here... as I have done no wrong in the eyes of my Saviour Jesus Christ'....

(MARY draws loud gasps and groans from the people around the room by holding up the crucifix with the body of Jesus Christ depicted on the cross).

(CECIL delivers what the official transcript of the trial describes as 'an historical discourse' of the Babington

Plot.
He argues point by point that she knows about the plot, approved of it, assented to it, promised her assistance and showed the ways and means).

CECIL
........' Madam you have been embroiled with a murderous band of traitors ...led by Anthony Babington ...to murder our most gracious majesty Queen Elizabeth... and we have letters from you ...
(Pause.. pointing at Mary)... conspiring with others to participate in this heinous act of treason of which you are guilty'....

(One of MARY's objections to the court's legitimacy was that its procedure is that of a treason trial.
She is not allowed a lawyer, she is not able to call any witnesses, and she is not allowed to use notes or examine

any documents in the course of conducting her own defence)

(MARY rises from her chair and exclaims loudly and angrily),

MARY
......' How can I be guilty of treason... I am not a subject of England... or my sister Elizabeth, ...however I am the grand-daughter of King Henry VII of

England,... and Queen of Scotland... and was Queen of France... until the death of my beloved husband Francis....I knew not Babington.... I never received any letters from him,... nor wrote any to him.... I never plotted the destruction of Queen ELIZABETH. ...If you want to prove it,.... then produce my letters signed by my own hand...(Pause)....

(Council CECIL replies irritably)...

CECIL
.....' But we have evidence of letters between you and Babington'....

(MARY still standing told him vexatiously holding her hands out) .....

MARY
.....' If so,.. why do you not produce them? ...I have a right to demand to see the originals and the copies side by side.... It is quite possible that my ciphers have been tampered with by my enemies .... I cannot reply to this accusation without full knowledge....
...... Until then,.... I must content myself with affirming solemnly that I am not guilty of the crimes imputed to me'....

(The council CECIL then produces a facsimile...waiving it above his head.... it had been 're-ciphered' from the 'lost'

original letter that was produced by
WALSINGHAM.
The facsimile was perfect and looks like
the original letter but it was not and
therefore should have been
in-admissible).
(MARY turns to her left to question
WALSINGHAM and tells him angrily),

MARY

...' It was an easy matter to counterfeit
the ciphers and characters of others,...
and all a forger had to do was to consult
my lately purloined... 'alphabet of
ciphers'... to discover the codes,...
assuming he did not ready know them'.

(WALSINGHAM rises to defend himself in his
usual slow manner);

WALSINGHAM

'I call God to record... that as a private
person I have done nothing unbeseeming an
honest man,... nor as I bear the place of
a public person have I done anything
unworthy of my place...
I have attempted no-one's death,... but I
am a faithful servant to my mistress Queen
Elizabeth,.. and I confess to being ever
vigilant.. in all that concerns the
safety of my Queen and Country...
Therefore I am watchful of all
conspirators'

(Under the pressure of the proceeding and surroundings MARY by this time is brought to tears she cries out)

              MARY
' I would never make shipwreck of my soul... by conspiring the destruction of my dearest sister'.

(The JUDGE bangs his gavel then stands up he is at the centre of the long table and tells the court),

              JUDGE
'We will now adjourn for lunch'.

(Everyone stands and Mary is escorted back to her room by her friend Melville she is still upset and wiping her eyes with her handkerchief).

In her room she picks up her little Skye terrier and whispers to the small dog

              MARY
Mon petit ange, le diable essaie de voler mon âme de vous'
' My little angel the devil is trying to steal my soul'

(The court resumes after dinner. Everyone resumes their places and MARY takes her seat).

(Prosecuting council CECIL stands up he exclaims loudly to the court looking from left to right, then direct at MARY)

                    CECIL
'My Lords and Gentlemen,... Madam,... Babington confessed to your involvement and knowledge of the plot'

(MARY jumps up and shouts angrily)

                    MARY
' Where is he...?.. then let him speak the truth in front of me and the court... and let me ask him about these letters of conspiracy'.

       (The prosecuting council still standing replies irritably)

                    CECIL
'I am afraid this request is impossible... as he was executed for treason... along with the other conspirators'

(MARY moves forward to the table and shouts back at him)

                    MARY

' This is very convenient... that you no doubt extracted anything you wanted from Babington... under torture... to bring me to this court and expect me to defend the allegations of treason... against myself whilst I have no recourse to examine the witnesses against me'....

(The council CECIL replies acidly)

CECIL
' Madam... we have the incriminating letters we took from Babington that you sent to him....
...With court's permission I shall read this letter';

(CECIL picks up a letter from the table he reads out loud very slowly and pausing frequently between every line to create maximum effect)

CECIL
'These are your words (Pointing at MARY)
'Thank you... to my friends for your care how to enlarge our liberty,... to restore us to our rightful seat, to cease our daily griefs,... to suppress our usurping and undeserved foes,... to quench the rage of erroneous tyrants,.. to the furtherance of God's word,.. to the releasement of Christians.

...What works could be more acceptable to

God... than to succor the Catholic
Church,... to defend the rightful title of
a prince,... to deliver afflicted
Christians from bondage,... and to restore
justice to all men,... by cutting of the
most faithless Antichrist and'...

(Loud gasps and angry shouts around the
room)

BACKGROUND VOICES
...'Shame on the Scottish Queen... for
calling our majesty the Antichrist'

(The council CECIL holds up his hand to
bring order and continues reading the
letter more slowly and pronounced and
repeating the last line)

CECIL
....'to restore justice to all men,... by
cutting of the most faithless
Antichrist... and usurper of titles, the
destroyer of justice,... the persecutor of
God and his Church,... the disturber of all
quiet states,... the only maintainer of
all seditious and mischievous rebels of
God and all Catholic princes'.....

(Shouts of anger rise up all around the
room the commissioners are banging their
fists on the table and throwing papers in
the air)

                    BACKGROUND VOICES
'Treason, treason this is a disgrace death to the Scottish bastard'.

(The council holds the letter shaking it wildly in his hand and waits till quiet had resumed)

(He says calmly)

                          CECIL
...'My Lords and Gentlemen... I have more to read here from this damning document of the highest treason... against ...our majesty Queen Elizabeth,... pray allow me to continue'.

(MARY stands up and defiantly replies),

                          MARY
'This was not written by mine hand as God is my witness'.

(The JUDGE bangs his gavel on the table and shouts)

                          JUDGE
'Order,... order...order,.. be seated madam... and keep your silence until asked to speak'

(MARY replies angrily looking to the JUDGE at the centre of the table)

MARY
...'I will not keep silent... on the face of a parcel of lies... being propagated about me without my right to see this letter in my hand... to examine it... as I have been refused council to defend me... or for me to take any notes in my defence...

...This is not a court of law or justice...indeed this is a corruption of decency...what is the point of me being here if I cannot speak for myself...and to defend my honour....then who will?'.

(MARY sits down quite exhausted, wiping her mouth with her handkerchief then sipping some water)

(The JUDGE then turns to the council when the room became silent, he says)

JUDGE
'Please continue councillor'

(The council CECIL stands up, coughs and starts to read the letter from the last line)

CECIL
'Thank you your honour...The accused wrote...
...'The disturber of all quiet states,..

the only maintainer of all seditious and mischievous rebels of God and all Catholic princes,... having a way made by our Holy Father'...

(Shouts of abuse go up)

BACKGROUND VOICES
'Damn the Holy Father of Rome he is the greatest enemy of England'.

(The council CECIL continues to read)

CECIL
...'Wherefore we beseech you to proceed in God's name and our Blessed Lady's... with the assistance of the whole company'.

(After these returns damaging statements are read out of confessions from MARY's secretaries.

(CECIL reading from some notes)

CECIL
...' Madam...your secretaries...Jaques Nau... and Gilbert Curle have admitted... that you wrote these letters when Sir Francis Walsingham questioned them

recently,... after the traitor Babington was executed as he admitted to having contact with them'

(MARY stands up and says)

MARY
'The majesty and safety of all princes falleth to the ground... if they depend upon the writings and testimony of their secretaries,... I am not to be convicted... except by mine own word or writing'.

(She points out sharply to the court)

MARY
...'My secretaries had not been called as witnesses... and so could not be cross-examined'.

(She also observes)

...'My initial memo of rough headings for the letters I had discussed with my secretaries... on the crucial day had disappeared...
....I am forced to defend myself without... being allowed to subject any of the documents... exhibited against me to legal or forensic scrutiny,... where are my secretaries now?'....

(CECIL looks to his right at WALSINGHAM

frowning, he stands up and replies)

CECIL

' For their own safety... and the safety of our majesty Queen Elizabeth,... we have them in a secure place,... ...in The Tower of London'

(MARY cries out in anguish)

MARY

...'Please don't harm them.... they have committed no wrong against my sister Elizabeth.'

(CECIL replies angrily)

CECIL

...'Not only do we have Depositions from your secretaries Jaques Nou... and Gilbert Curle,... but also from your Jesuit priest friend.... John Ballard... and Anthony Babington... and John Savage... and Chidock Tichbourn... and Robert Barnwell... and Thomas Salisbury... and Henry Doon,... who all... admitted to being involved to assassinate... our majesty Queen Elizabeth... and to over throw the government of England... with the help of your Ambassador the Bishop of Glasgow... who is based in Paris....

They had also been in communication with the Spanish King... to send an army to England... and to enthrone you as the Queen of England....

Do you deny these accusations... do you admit to knowing Anthony Babington... and the Jesuit John Ballard... who was leading a campaign to overthrow the throne of England... with force from Catholic Spain.

(MARY stands up and walks to the table holding her hands out then to her breast)

MARY

'Yes I deny these accusations...it is easy for you to say you confessions of men who were tortured...now executed.......Execution seems to be a great pastime for the English ...throne and my sister Elizabeth the Queen of England...she seems to have adopted her father Henry VIII...and his taste for brutality particularly against innocent women...now I also stand alone...

......against the brutality of the Tudor taste for blood'....

BACKGROUND VOICES

'Shame on this traitorous Mary of Scots...away with her head'...

(Judge banging his gavel)

JUDGE

'Order...order...order...Madam...you are

out of order if you continue with this type of rhetoric I will have to remove you. Carry on council CECIL'...

CECIL

'Thank you your honour I presume that everyone knows now the thoughts of the accused....

...We knew all about Ballard after completing his training as a Jesuit priest,... he returned to England as....

...a Catholic missionary and,... as such,.. had a price on his head.... In order to conceal his true identity, he played the part of a swashbuckling,... courtly soldier called Captain Fortescue...he was sent by the Jesuits with the sanction of The Pope in Rome.

...He was once described as wearing... 'a fine cape laced with gold,... a cut satin doublet and silver buttons on his hat'...

Being a tall, dark-complexioned man,... he was referred to by those who were unaware of his true identity as... 'Black Foskew'...

...In Babington's plot Ballard instigated... Chidiock_ and others to assassinate our gracious majesty Queen

Elizabeth... as a prelude to a full-blown invasion of ...England by Spanish-led

Catholic forces.

However,... the plot had been discovered and nurtured by Sir FRANCIS WALSINGHAM from the start.

...Indeed,... Ballard's inseparable companion and fixer,... Barnard Maude,... who travelled everywhere with him, was actually a DOUBLE AGENT FOR US'....

(MARY trembling but she stands her ground and says in a defiant attitude)

MARY

...'It is true I have known Anthony Babington.. as he was a page for me many years ago...
...But I did not know John Ballard... and I cannot be held responsible for the Jesuit Order,... as they only answer to the Holy Father in Rome... and as I believe their duty is to restore the Catholic Church to England...
....No one with any sanity can accuse me of instigating the Jesuits... as they are the front line fighters of the Faith... I am a captive woman being held in prisons if you feel you have a problem with the actions of the Jesuits... then why do not you arrest the Pope... and put him on trial'?...

(CECIL shatteringly interrupts)

CECIL
'I must remind you that Babington admitted to passing letters onto you through the empty beer casks... where the hidden letters were intercepted by Mr Walsingham's agents'.
(MARY turns to the judge and the rest of the councilors shaken but putting on a frown)

MARY
'Gentlemen, you must understand that I am no longer ambitious.... I wish for nothing but to pass my days in tranquility... I am too old now, too infirm to wish to rule'

(CECIL storms back shouting)

CECIL
'You have continuously asserted your pretensions to the throne of England'

(MARY quietly but sternly retorts cryptically)

MARY
'I have never given up asserting my rights for freedom and justice and equality and my belief in my Catholic Faith'.

(She points to WALSINGHAM and cries angrily)

MARY

'You are my enemy you have falsely laid plans to entrap me with lies and accusations you cannot present...

 I know about the dreadful torture you imposed on these men who you say accused me...

 Anyone will say anything under your devilish hideous torture to escape the pain.

I have never sought to harm my sister Elizabeth the Queen of England,... I would rather one hundred times and more have given my life than to see so many Catholics suffer for my sake,.. such is happening in this evil regime today under the dictatorship of you and Baron Cecil... You are both the enemies of the people of England and humanity and my Lord Jesus Christ.'

(WALSINGHAM angrily jumps up and retorts)

WALSINGHAM

'No true subject of the Queen was ever put to death on account of religion,... though some have died for

treason and because they maintained the Bull of Excommunication against our Queen and majesty Elizabeth,.. those who accepted the authority of the Pope and the Catholic Church against her.

(MARY still standing replies conflictingly)

MARY

' I have heard contrary to this to be so... and everyone in the Christian world knows what you say is an untruth,... as Catholics have and are still being persecuted and murdered not only here in England... but in my realm of Scotland and in Ireland and Wales... the persecution is without bounds and limits.

...I am not responsible for the actions of my sister Elizabeth's Excommunication... as I believe she had the opportunity to reconcile with the Pope... and he re-issued the Bull... 'In Cena Domini'... in 1568 while I was living in Scotland,... and Elizabeth was fully Excommunicated by the Bull... 'Regnans in Excelsis'... in 1570... and as I and all the world know... this absolves all her subjects from allegiance to her,... am I to be blamed for her actions and the actions of the Pope?

BACKGROUND VOICE

' This is an outrage she has condemned herself enough of her blasphemy and traitorous words she is an enemy of England and our Queen away with her'

(The JUDGE bangs his gavel on the table several times calling out)

JUDGE
'Order, order, order, Madam please confine your answers to the court... and not on what you imagine or supposed hearsay... as you have no proof of what you are saying,

(Mary turns her attention to CECIL opposite her and demands)

MARY
'Why do you not bring my secretaries, Nau and Gilbert Curle to give evidence in my presence.... If you continue to believe and ask the court to continue to believe that they would continue to condemn me... you would not hesitate to have brought them face to face with me.
This because you are afraid of the truth being told in my presence... and the presence of the Gentlemen sitting in judgment of me... in this apology for justice and truth....

(CECIL stands up shakily and in a quivering voice replies)

CECIL
' This is unnecessary... as Mr. WALSINGHAM has required statements from them and for me this is justice and truth'

(WALSINGHAM calls out loudly)

WALSINGHAM
' Hear, hear truth will win the day'.

(At this point MARY throws her seat cushion at him and screams at him)

MARY
'I have had enough of your concocted lies and abominations against me..., I am leaving'...

(She moves unsteadily and pushes her chair back.. and it falsl to the floor... and she storms out of the hall, her assistant Melville takes her arm to guide and steady her she turns before she goes through the door and calls out loudly and aggressively)

MARY
'I see now the kind of trail you gave to my Scottish kinsman William Wallace.... and I know about the justice you gave to

him... for being a faithful servant of Scotland,... I am not afraid of anyone here... and I will fight for my dignity and my faith.... I will never

be defeated... and as Jesus Christ is my Lord and God.. I am prepared to die without fear'....

(Several guards follow her as she leaves the room)

(The JUDGE bangs his gavel and calls out)

JUDGE
'We will adjourn until the morn'

(The debate continues late into the evening with councillors).

END OF SCENE 2

(CURTAIN)

Scene 3

(MARY is escorted back to her room with Melville and picks up her little dog crying and kissing her pet. Melville says to her)

MELVILLE
'I will bring you some food Your Majesty,... you must eat something as you have not ate for 3 days... and you need all your strength for this battle'

(MARY replies tearfully)

MARY
'Thank you my dear friend... but I have no appetite for food,... but perhaps I can try some soup and bread, then I will try to sleep as I am exhausted,... have you something you can bring for my sweet little baby?

(Melville says affectionately)
 'Certes, votre majesté, je reviendrai très bientôt'

(CECIL and WALSINGHAM retire from the court to Cecil's private apartment come-office WALSINGHAM says)

WALSINGHAM
'I am sure we have her now for sure... and on the morrow...we can present the Babington letter in full... and her letter of reply to Babington'.

(CECIL replies sharply and with venom)

CECIL
'This is a highly intelligent woman we are dealing with here,... why did you not keep the original letter she sent in cypher to show the court?..

WALSINGHAM
'I could not as this would have aroused her suspicions if her original letter did not get to Babington... and ...they would all have escaped... and my spies would have been exposed and no doubt killed,... so we had to copy her letter and let it go through.

CECIL (retorts)
'Don't forget I still have to take this to the Parliament... and ELIZABETH... to get their consent to execute this damn woman,... regardless of the outcome of this trial here'

WALSINGHAM
' We can also use the murder of her husband Lord Darnley against her... as she was implicated with her next husband the Earl of Bothwell,... and we could claim her reason for being involved with the murder of Darnley... was because he killed her secretary Rizzio.. and she took revenge on Darnley'

CECIL
'Yes we must use everything to defame her in anyway we can...
But you and I know that the Earl of Morton was executed in Scotland 6 years ago by the Scottish Court... for the murder of Darnley,... and John Knox was involved in the murder of Rizzio,... ah... these Scots are a damnation upon us all,... however... we will use everything... as no doubt it will add more spice to our case in defaming this intolerable woman,... who will bring

about our doom if we fail this quest....
...Good night I will see you on the morrow'

(CURTAIN)

Scene 4

Saturday 15th October;
Mary faces the might of the English legal minds as she stands alone without council or friend, with only her crucifix in her hand to comfort her, in the vast hall at Fotheringhay
surrounded by hundreds of angry faces baying for her death.

(CECIL opens the proceedings by addressing the court)

CECIL
'My Lords and Gentlemen,... I will bring to the attention of the court the letters written by Anthony Babington... to the defendant Marie Stuart... and the letter written by her... to Babington.

These letters will no doubt bring about a guilty verdict... before this day is out'

(The case turned immediately onto whether she had consented to Elizabeth's assassination and the court's insistence that the copied letter to Babington proposed the execution of the queen).

(MARY contended that the circumstances of the case against her might be proved but never the fact).

(MARY stood up looking around the room and said)

MARY
' My Lords and Gentlemen... my argument is that I must point to the letter... even though it was a facsimile... that there was no indication that I had planned the assassination of Elizabeth'.

(CECIL lifted the letter and called out)

CECIL

'My Lords and Gentlemen... with the permission of the court... I will read the letter from Anthony Babington to the accused...... this letter was intercepted by Mr. Walsingham's agents.

CECIL

'Most mighty,.. most excellent,.. my dread sovereign Lady and Queen, unto whom only I owe all fidelity and obedience....

...It may please your gracious Majesty to admit the excuse of my long silence and discontinuance from the dutiful offices incepted....

...Upon the remove of your royal person from the ancient place of your abode to the custody of a wicked puritan... and mere Leicestrian,... a mortal enemy both.....

......by faith and faction to your Majesty and the State Catholic,.. I held the hope of our country's weal depending next under God upon the life and health of your Majesty to be desperate,.. and thereupon resolved to depart the land, determining to spend the remainder of my life in such solitary sort as the wretched and miserable state of my country did require,.. daily expecting ...

(according to the just judgment of God).. the deserved confusion thereof, which Our Lord for His mercy's sake prevent...

...The which my purpose being in execution, and standing upon my departure, there was addressed to me from the parts beyond the seas one Ballard,... a man of virtue and learning and of singular zeal to the Catholic cause and your Majesty's service...

BACKGROUND VOICES

'Damn the Catholic cause and death to all traitors...

(JUDGE banging his gavel)

JUDGE

'Order...order...order..please resume council CECIL'...

CECIL

'Thank you your honour...if the court will allow me to continue...these are the words written by Babington to the accused...this is where I stopped ...he stated...

...This man informed me of great preparation by the Christian princes... (your Majesty's allies)... for the deliverance of our country... from the extreme and miserable state wherein it hath too long remained: ...

...Which when I understood,... my special desire was to advise by what means, with the hazard of my life and..

....friends in general,.. I might do your sacred Majesty one good day's service...

...Whereupon, most dear Sovereign,.. according to the great care which those princes have of the preservation and safe delivery of your Majesty's sacred person,... I advised of means and considered of the circumstances according to the weight of the affair:... and after long consideration and conference had with so many the wisest and most trusty as with safety I might commend the secrecy thereof unto, I do find... (by the assistance of Our Lord Jesus)... assurance of good effect and desired fruit of our travails.

(CECIL paused to take a drink and mop his brow and said)

(MARY exceptionally agitated)

MARY

'This is so ridiculous...all you have are forged letters...and I am expected to sit and listen to a pack of lies being read out without my intervention being heard...This is a trial for my life...and you have all reached an agreement that I am to be strung out...this is a very conspicuous conspiracy to consume my soul.'...

CECIL

' Please allow me to continue...Babington wrote to you'...

'These things are first to be advised in this great and honorable action, upon the issue of which depend not only the life of your most excellent Majesty...

...(which God long preserve to our inestimable comfort and to the salvation of English souls)... and the life...

....of all us actors herein, but also the honour and weal of our country,... far than our lives more dear to us, and the last hope ever to recover the faith of our forefathers... and to redeem ourselves from the servitude and bondage which heresy hath imposed upon us with the loss of thousands of souls:

First,.... assuring of invasion:..

...Sufficient strength in the invader:..

...Ports to arrive at appointed, with a strong party at every place to join with them and warrant their landing...

...The deliverance of your Majesty...

The dispatch of the usurping Competitor....

..For the effectuating of all which it may please your Excellency to rely upon my service.....

MARY protested angrily

MARY

'I cannot be held responsible for this letter or any other letter written about me or to me... by people I know not in person and who have any desire to organize invasion or wars,... my only desire is to obtain my freedom not to do harm to anyone on God's earth'...

(CECIL retorted sharply)

CECIL

'Madam,... Please do not interrupt me as I am reading the words of Babington to the court you may have your...

....reply when I finish this correspondence,... if I may continue'....

(He looked towards the JUDGE, the JUDGE motioned with his hand and said)

JUDGE

' Please continue council CECIL'

(CECIL started to read from the letter)

CECIL

...'I vow and protest before the face of Almighty God... (Who miraculously hath long preserved your sacred person, no doubt to some universal good end) that what I have said shall be performed,.... or all our lives happily lost in the execution thereof;.. which vow all the chief actors herein have taken solemnly and are, upon assurance by your Majesty's letters unto me,.. to receive the Blessed Sacrament thereupon,.. either to prevail in the Church's behalf and your Majesty's, or fortunately to die for that honourable cause.....

...Now forasmuch as delay is extreme dangerous,.... it may please your most excellent Majesty by your wisdom ...to direct us,.. and by your princely authority to enable such as may advance the affair;.. foreseeing that, where is not any of the nobility at liberty assured to your Majesty in this desperate service...

..(except unknown to us).. and seeing it is very necessary that some there be to become heads to lead the multitude, ever disposed by nature in this land to follow nobility,... considering withal it doth not only make the commons and gentry to follow without contradiction or contention ...(which is ever found in....

....equality) but also doth add great courage to the leaders.... For which necessary regard I recommend some unto your Majesty as fittest in my knowledge for to be your Lieutenants in the West parts,... in the North parts,... South Wales,... North Wales.. and the Counties of Lancaster,... Derby... and Stafford:.. all which countries, by parties already made and fidelities taken in your Majesty's name,... I hold as most assured and of most undoubted fidelity. ..

...Myself with ten gentlemen.... and a hundred of our followers... will undertake the delivery of your royal person from the hands of your enemies.....

(MARY interrupts him saying)

MARY....

"I came into this kingdom under promise of assistance,... and aid,... against my enemies and not as a subject,... as I could prove to you had I my papers;... instead of which I have been detained and imprisoned... I do not deny that I have earnestly wished for liberty... and done my utmost to procure it for myself.....

...In this I acted from a very natural wish...Can I be responsible for the criminal projects of a few desperate men,.... which they planned without my knowledge or participation?"

(CECIL exasperated said),

CECIL

'Madam may I proceed'

(He continues to read the letter)

'For the dispatch of the usurper,... from the obedience....

.....of whom we are by the excommunication of her made free, there be six noble gentlemen,.... all my private friends,... who for the zeal they bear to the Catholic cause..... and your Majesty's service will undertake that tragic execution.....

(Loud shouts rang around the hall)

BACKGROUND VOICES

'Death to all Catholic devils, damnation

be upon the Scottish Queen'

(The JUDGE called while banging his gavel)

JUDGE

' Order, Order, Order, I will have the court cleared if we do not have order, continue council CECIL'

(CECIL was smiling and enjoying his stirring speech , he continued reading the letter)

CECIL

...'It resteth that,... according to their infinite good deserts and your Majesty's bounty, their heroic attempt may be honorable rewarded in them,... if they escape with life,... or in their posterity, and that so much I may be able by your Majesty's authority to assure them.

Now it remaineth only that by your Majesty's wisdom it ...may be reduced into method:... that your happy deliverance be first, for that thereupon dependeth our only good;... and that all the other circumstances so concur that the untimely beginning of one end do not overthrow the rest....

...All which your Majesty's wonderful experience and...

....wisdom will dispose of in so good manner as I doubt not, through God's good assistance,... all shall come to desired effect; for the obtaining of which every one of us shall think his life most happily spent.

...Upon the sixth of this month... I will be at Lichfield, expecting your Majesty's answer and letters,.... in readiness to execute what by them shall be commanded....

...Your Majesty's most faithful subject and sworn servant,...

...Anthony Babington

(CECIL paused for a few seconds... looked around the hall then said)

CECIL

...'This part is addressed to Jaques Nau the personal secretary of the accused....

...To Mr. Nau, Secretary to her Majesty.... Mr. Nau, I would gladly understand what opinion you hold of one Robert Poley,... whom I find to have intelligence of her Majesty's occasions.... I am private with the man, and by means thereof know somewhat, but suspect more... I pray you deliver your opinion of him....

(MARY interrupts saying)

MARY

"Nau had many peculiarities,... likings and intentions that I cannot mention in public...

For my part, I do not wish to accuse my secretaries, but I can see plainly that what they have said is from fear of torture and death....

Under promise of their lives and in order to save themselves,... they have accused themselves at my expense,... fancying that I could thereby more easily save myself,... at the same time, not knowing where I was, and not suspecting the manner in which I am treated...

If they were in my presence now they would clear me on the spot of all blame... and would have put me out of case."

(CECIL sits down, there are more noises around the hall and the JUDGE bangs his gavel calling out)

JUDGE

'We will adjourn for lunch and return at 2 o'clock'

(People all around the hall were talking)

(MARY leaves the hall escorted by Melville back to her room).

(CECIL and WALSINGHAM go to CECIL's room.)

(CURTAIN)

SCENE 5

(MARY lays on her bed and her little dog jumps up beside her and she cuddles the dog. Melville says)

MELVILLE

'I will bring some cheese and fruit Your Majesty ..would you like something more substantial?'.

(MARY just sighs softly)

MARY

'Non...Merci mon cher ami..I am very tired and we have only just begun this battle for my life...against all these lies and false accusations...from those despicable devils... CECIL and WALSINGHAM'

(CECIL and WALSINGHAM are very smug and happy CECIL laughs and pats him on his back saying)

CECIL

'I see we have all the people with us... and when I read out her letter... she will be doomed and we will have the bitch's head on a plate'

(WALSINGHAM)

'Yes my Lord and we must also bring in the murder of Darnley... to put the nail into her coffin.'

(CURTAIN)

SCENE 6

(The court resumes with everyone in place)
(CECIL standing starts to speak)

CECIL

'My Lords and Gentlemen... with the court's permission I will read this letter that was written by the accused to Anthony Babington'.

(MARY jumps up and shouts at him putting her hands onto her head)

MARY

'This is not any letter written by me... this is a copy written by Walsingham's agent... any letters I have written are in my own hand'.

(The JUDGE asks CECIL)

JUDGE

'Is this a facsimile if so... where is the original'?

(CECIL retorts)

CECIL

'Your honour... the original letter was written in cypher by the accused... and had to be forwarded to Babington... otherwise the plot would have been compromised... and our agent would have been exposed... ...if we did not let her cyphered letter pass on.... and if we did not capture Babington's associates... they could and would have assassinated out Gracious

Majesty Queen Elizabeth..... Babington destroyed the original written by the hand of this woman who sits before me'...

(He points at MARY)

JUDGE

'Very well council, carry on'.

(MARY shouts in anger
MARY
C'est un outrage à la justice et de liberté qui tache à jamais l'Angleterre

JUDGE

'Please sit down Madam,.... I have given my permission for the letter to be read by the council..... Carry on council proceed with the letter'

(Cecil picks up the letter and starts to read, he says)
CECIL

'Thank you your honour,... the letter the accused wrote starts...

...Trusty and well-beloved,... According to the zeal and entire affection which I have known in you towards the common cause of religion and mine,.... having always made account of you as of a principal and right worthy member to be employed both in the one and the other:.. it hath been no less consolation unto me to understand your estate as I have done by your last,.... and to have found means to renew my intelligence with you,... than I have felt grief all this while past to be without the same. I pray you therefore from henceforth to write unto me so often as you can of all occurrences which you may judge in any wise important to the good of my affairs,.. whereunto I shall not fail to correspond with all the care and diligence that

shall be in my possibility'...

(MARY breaks in pleadingly)

MARY

"I do not desire vengeance.... I leave it to Him.... who is the just Avenger... of the innocent and of those who suffer for His Name... under whose power I will take shelter.... I would rather pray with Esther than take the sword with Judith...."

(CECIL carries on reading the letter)

CECIL

...'For divers great and important considerations... (which were here too long to be deduced)... I cannot but greatly praise and commend your common desire to prevent in time the designments of our enemies.... for the extirpation of our religion out of this realm with the ruin of us all...

....For I have long ago shown unto the foreign Catholic princes—and experience doth approve it—the longer that they and we delay to put hand on the matter on this side,... the greater leisure have our said enemies to prevail and win advantage over the said princes ...

.... (as they have done against the King of Spain).... and in the meantime the Catholics here,... remaining exposed to all sorts of persecution and cruelty,... do daily diminish in number,... forces,... means and power....

So as,.. if remedy be not thereunto hastily provided, I fear not a little but they shall become altogether unable for ever to rise again and to receive any aid at all,... whensoever it were offered them.

(MARY is distressed and standing up shakily saying)

MARY

"I cannot walk without assistance nor use my arms,... and I spend most of my time confined to bed by sickness...

...My advancing age... and bodily weakness both prevent me from wishing to resume the reins of government...

...I have perhaps only two or three days to live in this world,... and I do not aspire to any public position, especially when I consider the pain and ...desperance which meet those who wish to do right..., and act with justice and dignity in the midst of so perverse a generation,... and when a whole world is full of crimes and troubles..."

(The JUDGE bangs his gavel saying)

JUDGE

'Madam, please allow the council to proceed'

(CECIL turns to the JUDGE saying)

'Thank you your honour',

CECIL

'For mine own part,... I pray you to assure our principal friends that, albeit I had not in this cause any particular interest...

(that which I may pretend unto being of no consideration unto me in respect of the public good of this state)... I shall be always ready and most willing to employ therein my life and all that I have or may ever look for in this world.

...Now,... for to ground substantially this enterprise and to bring it to good success,.. you must first examine deeply:... What forces,... as well on foot as on horse,.. you may raise amongst you all,... and what Captains you shall appoint for them in every shire,.. in case a chief

general cannot be had.... Of what towns,... ports and havens you may assure yourselves,... as well in the North,.. West as South,... to receive succors from the Low Countries,... Spain and France....

(MARY interrupts him crying out)

MARY

...'This a complete concoction of lies...lies...lies'

(CECIL continues to read, ignoring MARY)

CECIL

> 'What place you esteem fittest and of greatest advantage to assemble the principal company of your forces at:... and the same being assembled, whether or which way you have to march. ..

...What foreign forces, as well on horse as foot, you require...

(which would be compassed conform to the proportion of yours),... for how long paid, and munition and ports the fittest for their landing in this realm from the three aforesaid foreign countries...

What provision of money and Armour (in case you want) you would ask.

By what means do the six gentlemen deliberate to proceed?

And the manner also of my getting forth of this hold'.

(MARY stands up and objected she says sympathetically with her hands together as in a prayer)

...'MY Lords and Gentlemen.... all of you sitting in this court today know of me and my captivity for over 20.... years and my desperation to secure my freedom... and liberty....

I have to defend myself against this forged letter... without having the opportunity to take notes... or have legal representation....

I make no apology for contacting my friends... and supporters... in other nations have I not this right.... Many people want me to be free... as I have committed no crime against anyone'....

(CECIL interrupts causticly)

'Madam if I may continue you will have your chance to speak when I have finished reading your letter'

MARY (replies sharply)

'I must remind you sir... that this letter you read is the fiction produced by Mr. WALSINGHAM

(CECIL starts to read the letter talking over MARY)...

CECIL

...'The accused wrote....

...'Upon which points having taken amongst you (who are the principal authors,... and also as few in number as you can) the best resolution, my advice is that you impart the same with all diligence to Bernardino de Mendoza,... ambassador lieger for the

King of Spain in France,... who (besides the experience he hath of the estate of this side) I may assure you will employ him therein most willingly....

> .....I shall not fail to write unto him of the matter with all the earnest recommendations that I can;... as I shall also to any else that shall be needful...
>
> (MARY stood up and looked around the hall pleading)...

MARY

"There is not one,... I think,... among you, let him be the cleverest man you will,... but would be incapable of resisting or defending himself were he in my place...."

Cecil

'Madam...if you could be so kind as to let me continue...these are your words...not mine or Sir Francis Walsingham's......'But you must make choice, for managing of this affair with the said Mendoza and others out of the realm,... of some faithful and very secret personage,... unto whom only you must commit yourselves, to the end things be the more secret,.. which for your own security I recommend unto you above the rest. ..

(MARY breaks in sharply)...

MARY

'These are not my words...these are a fictional corruption of truth...

CECIL   (Angry)

'Madam....this is your letter...my Lords and Gentlemen...these are her words...

...'If your messenger bring you back again sure promise and sufficient assurance of the succor you demand..., then thereafter...

(but no sooner, for that it were in vain)... take diligent order that all those of your party on this side make... (so secretly as they can) provision of Armour,... fit horse.. and ready money,...

(Interruption from BACKGROUND VOICES)

'We need to hear no more she is guilty and damned'

CECIL (reading impatiently)...

....'wherewith to hold themselves in

readiness... to march so soon as it shall be signified unto them by their chief and principals in every shire...

...And for the better colouring of the matter ...

(reserving to the principal the knowledge of the ground of the enterprise) ...it shall be enough,... for the beginning, to give out to the rest that the said provisions are made only for fortifying yourselves,...

in case of need, against the puritans of this realm:...

...the principal whereof, having the chief forces of the same in the Low Countries,.. have

...(as you may let the bruit go)... designed to ruin and overthrow, at their return home,... the whole Catholics,.... and to usurp the Crown;....

(Loud angry roars from BACKGROUND VOICES)

'This is an outrage death to all traitors,... God save Queen ELIZABETH'....

(CECIL SMILING AND ENJOYING HIS RANT goes ON)....

CECIL

...'not only against me and all other lawful pretenders thereunto, but against their own Queen that now is...if she will not altogether commit herself to their only government...

...The same pretexts may serve to sound and establish amongst you all an association and confederation general,... as done only for your own just preservations and defense,... as well in religion as in lives,.. lands and goods,... against the oppression and attempts of the said puritans,... without touching directly by writing anything against that Queen,... but rather showing yourselves willing to maintain her and her lawful heirs after her,... unnaming me....

MARY

..."He who does not keep faith where it is due,..will hardly keep it where it is not due."....

CECIL (Reading loudly)

....'The affairs being thus prepared and forces in readiness both without and within the realm,... then shall it be time to set the six gentlemen to work;....

(CECIL STOPS LOOKS AROUND THE ROOM THEN CONTINUES)...

CECIL

...'taking order,... upon the accomplishing of their designing, I may be suddenly transported out of this place,.... and that all your forces in the same time be on the field to meet me in tarrying for the arrival of the foreign aid,... which then must be hastened with all diligence.....

Now,.... for that there can be no certain day appointed for the accomplishing of the said gentlemen's designing,... to the end that others may be in readiness to take me from hence,... I would that the said gentlemen had always about them... (or at least at Court)... a four stout men,... furnished with good and speedy horses,.. for—so soon as the said design shall be executed—to come with all diligence to advertise thereof those that shall be appointed for my transporting;... to the end that immediately after they may be at the place of my abode,... before that my keeper can have advice of the execution of the said design,... or at least before he can fortify himself within the house or carry me out of the same....

...It were necessary to dispatch two or three of the said advertisers by divers ways,... to the end that, if the one be stayed, the other may come through;.. and at the same instant were it also needful to essay to cut off the posts ordinary ways.'...

(Interruption)

(Loud noises come from the far side of the hall and 2 guards run over to CECIL as someone in the audience has tried to rush a CECIL with a knife....but he has been tripped up by some of the other bystanders....2 guards went to the side of MARY.... the hall is in an uproar as the man is subjugated....everyone is standing at the long table....the man is dragged out....the JUDGE starts to bang his gavel...calling out)...

JUDGE

'Order...Order...Order'...

(WALSINHAM comes to the side of CECIL and whispered to him...this was a plan they had set up to add more drama...CECIL pats WALSINGHAM on the back..... MARY...is watching them closely and knows they had created this to make the case against her more damning...

....MARY-pointing..as she stands up and moves to the table, calling out at them in a rage)....

MARY

...'I see your evil doings here but you do not fool me,.... however you may fool everyone in this farce of a court...not only have you presented a lot of lies against me...but that is not enough for you scheming interrupters of truth... but you want to blacken me more with this charade'...

JUDGE (banging gavel and shouting)...

...'ORDER...ORDER...ORDER...Council CECIL can we have a few moments please in private'....

(CECIL and the JUDGE walk over to a corner to confab then goes back to his place at the table)

JUDGE

...'Madam... we can bring this to an end if you wish to plead guilty.;...

MARY

...'Plead guilty to treason?... how can I do this when I am not a subject of England....

am guilty of being a Catholic Queen,... if this is what you want... but I am innocent of all the lies portrayed against me.'...

JUDGE

'Please continue council CECIL.'..

CECIL

'Thank you your honour...The

accused wrote..

.....'This is the plan which I find best for this enterprise,... and the order whereby you should conduct the same for our common securities...

....For stirring on this side before you be well assured of sufficient foreign forces,... it were but for nothing to put yourselves in danger... of following the miserable fortune of such as have heretofore travailed in like occasions...

...And to take me forth of this place,.. un-being before well assured to set me in the midst of a good army,.. or in some very good strength where I may safely stay... on the assembly of your forces and arrival of the said foreign succours,... it were sufficient cause given to that Queen... in catching me again to enclose me forever in some hole,... forth of which I should never escape...

...(if she did use me no worse),... and to pursue with all extremity those that had assisted... me—which would grieve me more than all the unhap [which] might fall upon myself.'..

MARY

...."If I shall be holden here perforce,... you may be sure then being as a desperate person...

...I will use any attempts... that may serve my purpose either by myself or my friends. ..

...Do I not have the right as a Queen to fight for my freedom?'

CECIL (Angry)

...'Madam,... you had your freedom but you chose to come to England when you escaped from Scotland...now you are charged with writing these treacheries against our Queen...You wrote these words....

....'And therefore must I needs yet once again admonish you,... so earnestly as I can, to look and take heed most carefully and vigilantly,.. to compass and assure so well all that shall be necessary for the effectuating of the said enterprise,..

...as... (with the grace of God)... you may bring the same to happy end:..

...remitting to the judgment of our principal friends on this side, with whom you have to deal herein, to ordain [and] conclude upon this present...

..(which shall serve you only for an overture and proposition)... as you shall amongst you find best:.. and to yourself in particular I refer to assure the gentlemen above mentioned... of all that shall be requisite of my part for the entire execution of their good wills....

I leave also to your common resolutions to advise...

(in case their designment do not take hold, as may happen)... whether you will or not pursue my transport and the execution of the rest of the enterprise. ..

...But if the mishap should fall out that you might not come by me—being set in the Tower of London,... or in any other strength with greater ward, yet notwithstanding leave not,...for God's sake,... to proceed in the rest of the enterprise;... for I shall, at any time, die most contented,... understanding of your delivery forth of the servitude wherein you are holden as slaves....

....I shall assay that,.. at the same time that the work shall be in hand in these parts, to make the Catholics of Scotland arise and to put my son in their hands,...

MARY

..." You speak of my dearest son... I have borne him and God Knoweth with what danger to him and to me both,... and of you he is descended, so I mean not to forget my duty to you....

...He will someday rule over this realm... and return justice and avenge the cruelty that has been portrayed against me.....My sister Elizabeth is barren...

and now too old to bear a successor, my son will succeed her"

BACKGROUND VOICES

'This treasonable talk about our queen.'....

JUDGE..BANGING HIS GAVEL..

JUDGE

'Order-Order-Order....Madam... will you please sit down... and let the Council CECIL continue with reading this letter....Council CECIL please carry-on....

CECIL

'Thank you your honour...the letter of the accused states.....

....'To the effect that from thence our enemies here may not prevail of any succour.

I would also that some stirring in Ireland were laboured for,... and to be begun some while before anything were done here;... to the end the alarm might be given thereby on the flat contrary side that the stroke should come from....

MARY (Complaining)

...'This fiction is so ridiculous... as the whole world knows that the Catholics of Scotland... have been wiped out and only a handful are still left.'....

                CECIL (loudly)

'If I may continue Madam..... you wrote...

....Your reasons to have some general head or chief,... methinketh,.. are very pertinent; and therefore were it good to sound obscurely for the purpose the Earl of Arundel,... or some of his brethren,... and likewise to seek upon the young Earl of Northumberland,... if he be at liberty.

From over sea the Earl of Westmoreland may be had,... whose house and name may [do] much, you know, in the North parts:.... as also the Lord Paget,... of good ability in some shires hereabout;... both the one and the other may be brought home secretly:

            BACKGROUND VOICES..

'Treason...Treason...Treason...Westmoreland and his rebels must be caught...

         CECIL (Talking over the voices)

...amongst which some more of the principal banished may return, if the enterprise be once resolute.

The said Lord Paget is now in Spain, and may treat there all which, by his brother

Charles or directly by himself, you will commit unto him touching this affair.....

> MARY (Laughingly)

'This is utterly ridiculous as if I would be stupid enough to put into writing the names of my supporters.'...

> CECIL (Stiffens dignified)

'Madam...these are your words not mine...now if I may continue?....

....'Beware that none of your messengers, whom you sent forth of the realm,... carry over any letters upon themselves;... but make their dispatches be conveyed either after or before them, by some other...

Take heed of spies and false brethren that are amongst you—especially of some priests,... already practised by ...our enemies for your discovery;.. and in any wise....

....keep never any paper about you that in any sort may do harm....

> MARY (With dignity she stands to speak)

'My Lords and Gentlemen...surely you are all intelligent Gentlemen...if I had written such a letter as this...would I have needed to tell these men who to run their affairs on how to rescue me?...I presume that these men were all versed in their own minds... and plans... how they would put into action such a drastic eventually...According to CECIL and Walsingham's charade against me...the governments of Spain and France were supporting Babington and his associates...yet I am accused of writing a letter to tell these government agents how to conduct their business...this is so ridiculous that it beggars belief...that anyone would believe this fiasco presented here today...and I think that it is an insult to your intelligence to expect you to believe this nonsense....

        CECIL (Embarrassed and humiliated)

'My Lords and Gentlemen...I am not here today to defend myself and Sir Francis Walsingham's dignity...however..I am here today to bring a conviction of treasonable acts by the defendant...I can assure you these are her words that I read out to the court....she wrote...

...For from such like errors have come the only condemnation of all such as have suffered heretofore,... against whom could there otherwise have been nothing proved....

...Discover as little as you can your names and...

....intentions to the French Ambassador now lieger at London;... for although he be, as I understand, a very honest gentleman,... of good conscience and religion, yet fear I that his master entertaineth, with that Queen,.. a course far contrary to our designments;... which may move him to cross us,... if it should happen he had any particular knowledge thereof. ...

MARY

'I have been in contact the French Ambassador over many years...and I remember distinctly writing to him ....I can recall every word...I told him...

....Monsieur l'Ambassadeur,... if my preparation were not so much advanced as they are,... peradventure the Queen, your Mistress'... unkindness might stay my voyage;... but now I am determined to adventure the matter,.. whatsoever come of it; I trust the wind will be so favourable as I shall not need to come on the coast of England;.. and if I do,... Monsieur l'Ambassadeur,... the Queen your Mistress shall have me in her hands to do her will of me;... and if she be so hard-hearted... as to desire my end,... she may then do her pleasure,... and make sacrifice of me;... peradventure that casualty might be better for me than to live....

In this matter,.. God's will be

fulfilled."....

I was correct as I have been a prisoner of Elizabeth for 18 years.'... .

    CECIL (Proceeds reading with contempt)

...'All this while past I have sued to change and remove from this house; and, for answer,... the Castle of Dudley only hath been named to serve the turn.

So,.. as by appearance,.. within the end of this summer I may go thither....

Wherefore advise, so soon as I shall be there, what provision may be had about that part for my escape from thence....

If I stay here,... there is for that purpose but one of these three means following to be looked.... The first that at one certain day appointed,.. in my walking abroad on horseback on the moors betwixt this and Stafford... (where ordinarily you know very few people do pass),... a fifty or threescore men,... well horsed and armed,... come to take me there;... as they may easily,... my keeper having with him ordinarily but eighteen or twenty horsemen only with dags..

•   (MARY contests)

"Alas!.... Do not as the serpent that stoppeth his hearing,... for I am no enchanter but your sister and natural cousin of your Queen Elizabeth.... If Caesar had not disclaimed to hear or heed the complaint of an advertiser he had not so died...I am not of the nature of the basilisk and less of the chameleon,.. to turn you to my likeness."...

(CECIL continues to read)

..'The second mean is to come at midnight... (or soon after)... to set fire in the barns and stables,... which you know are near to the house; ...and whilst that my guardian's servants shall run forth to the fire,... your company ......(having everyone a mark whereby they may know one another under night)... might surprise the house;

...where I hope, with the few servants I have about me, I were able to give you correspondence. ..

And the third,... some that bring carts hither ordinarily coming early in the morning,... their carts might be so

prepared and with such cartleaders....
that being just in the middle of the great
gate the carts might fall down or
overwhelm, and that thereupon you might
come suddenly,... with your followers, to
make yourself master of the house,... and
carry me away....

So you might do safely,... before that any
number of soldiers... (who lodge in sundry
places forth of this place, some a half and
some a whole mile off)... might come to the
relief.'....

MARY (Interrupting angrily)

...'My Lords and Gentlemen this letter is
so absurd and total utter poppycock.... it
is beyond the belief of any sane person to
even imagine... that I would write the
names of friends... and draw out plans for
my ...escape on a letter that I knew could
be intercepted,...

am not some stupid imbecile and anyone of
you here today would know that I would
never compromise myself... or others in my
own hand...

I have known for several years that my
letters are read and examined,... and I
hope that you...

.....Gentlemen will realize... that I am not
stupid enough to have written such
rubbish'....

(CECIL was getting exasperated and shouted at her)

CECIL

....'Madam... I am at the end please be quiet and let me finish...you wrote...

...Whatever issue the matter taketh,... I do,... and will, think myself obliged, as long as I live,... towards you, for the offers you make to hazard yourself, as you do, for my delivery;...

...and by any means that ever I have,... I shall do my endeavor to recognise,... by effects,... your deserts herein....

...I have commanded a a more ample alphabet to be made for you,.. which herewith you will receive. ..

...God Almighty have you in protection.....

...Your most assured friend for ever, [Marie R.]

...Fail not to burn this present quickly.

..I would be glad to know the names and qualities of the six gentlemen... which are to accomplish the designment, for it may be I shall be able,... upon knowledge of the parties, to give you some further advice necessary to be followed therein,... as also ...from time to time particularly how you proceed, and as soon as you may... (for the same purpose) who be already, and how far,... everyone is privy hereunto. ...

'My Lords and Gentlemen.... this letter proves beyond doubt that the accused is guilty of treason... in

association with Anthony Babington's plot... to overthrow our gracious majesty Queen Elizabeth...

(CECIL looked around the hall and exclaimed loudly)

'My honourable Lords and Gentelmen....these are the destructive and treasonable acts pursued by the defendant...who is guilty of treason...and I request that you bring a guilty verdict against her... I rest my case'....

(MARY stood up and spoke softly, looking around the hall with her arms outstretched)

MARY
'My Lords and Gentlemen.... there is no mention in this ridiculous letter that I was involved in any conspiracy to assassinate my sister Elizabeth,... the entire letter is a fabrication of truth... created for the purpose of condemning me... and my friends and supporters....

...Where is the letter in my own hand?...

..It is certainly not here today in this court...

I am an independent Queen... and have been held in captivity here in England for 18 years... without ever being convicted of any wrongdoing....

...My only crime is that I am a Catholic Queen... and I believe in the True Faith of Jesus Christ... my Lord and my God...

From my point of view,... even an act of war was legitimate... if it allowed me to recover my freedom.

..If I was not an independent Queen,... then I am guilty....

...If I am,... and Elizabeth's death was no more than a providential incident... in my legitimate struggle to regain my rights,... I am innocent,.. this is how I see it.'...

(ELIZABETH's chief minister WILLIAM CECIL he tells MARY),

CECIL

...' All your failings and shortcomings in

your efforts to liberate yourself... were
the result of your own actions... and those
of the Scots who had betrayed you
and not of our majesty Queen Elizabeth'.

(On hearing this, MARY turns to him)

MARY
' Ah,.. I see your are my adversary....'

(CECIL replies),
' Yea, I am the adversary to Queen
Elizabeth's adversaries.... You were also
accused of being involved with the murder
of your husband Lord Darnley in Scotland'.

MARY
'You... and your friend Walsingham are
also adversary of young children....I also
have my agents who have informed me of your
devious perverted actions...

(Mary constantly stands her ground and
refuses to be intimidated and repeats),

MARY
' I will hear the proofs in another place
and defend myself....
...My Lords and Gentlemen,... it is known
to the world that the Earl of Morton was
tried and found guilty... and executed for
the foul murder of my husband,... my
cause is in the hands of God'.

(As the trail draws to a close the JUDGE asks)

JUDGE 'Madam... have you anything more you would like to say'?

(With great dignity and composure she replies),

MARY
' I again demand to be heard in a full Parliament,... or else speak personally to the Queen,... who would,.. I think, show more regard of another Queen...'.

With these words she stands up (as the official reporter notes) 'with great confidence of countenance',

(She speaks disparagingly to CECIL,and WALSINGHAM about her two secretaries,)

MARY (Angrily)
'This was a whole falsification of lies you presented against my secretaries... who were not allowed to be here'...

"I have desired nothing but my own

deliverance...my subjects became sad and haughty and abused my clemency;.. indeed they now complain that they were never so well off as under my government...

...My Lords and Gentlemen,... I place my cause in the hands of God...

May God keep me from having to do with you all again."

(MARY turns and she then sweeps out of the room escorted by Melville).

(CURTAIN)

That was the end of the trial.
The commissioners were ordered to reconvene on 25th October in the Star Chamber at Westminster

<u>End of Act 1</u>

ACT 2

SCENE 7

The scene is set in a luxurious palace in the large lavishly furnished office of Cecil who is sitting behind his large ornate desk.

There are several seats in front.

WALSINGHAM enters through the door with another man ushering him through.

(WALSINGHAM speaks excitedly to CECIL)

WALSINGHAM
....'My Lord,... we have the verdict from the Star Chamber at the Westminster Parliament....

...The principal Register Mr.Edward Barker is here with me... he would like to read out the result of the proceedings'.

(CECIL stands up and puts both hands on his desk. His face is set in an expression of frowning severity. He quickly replies)

CECIL
...'Carry on Mr. Barker read out the report'.

(Barker replies sternly)

BARKER

.."Thank you my Lord... these are the findings of the members at the Star Chamber on the proceedings against the Scottish Queen,... Mary Stuart.....

...The assembly was prorogued on the 25th of October
 1586, at the Star-Chamber at Westminster.

...By their joint assent and consent, they do pronounce and deliver their Sentence and Judgment,... at the day ...and ....place last recited; and say....

...That after the end of the aforesaid session of parliament, in the Commission aforesaid specified, namely after the aforesaid 1st day of June,... above said, and before the date of the same Commission, ...divers matters have been compassed and imagined within this realm of England,... by Anthony Babington and others,... Cum Scientia,... in English with the privity,... of the said Mary,... pretending title to the crown of this realm of England... tending to the hurt,... death and destruction of the royal person of our said Lady the Queen ELIZABETH....

..And namely,... That after the aforesaid

1st day of June,... in the 27th year above said, and before the date of the Commission aforesaid, the aforesaid Mary... pretending title to the crown of this realm of England,... hath compassed and imagined within this realm of England divers matters tending to the hurt,... death and destruction... of the royal person of our Sovereign Lady the Queen ELIZABETH,... contrary to the form of the statute in the Commission aforesaid specified." ...

(CECIL still standing claps his hands in joy and looking from WALSINGHAM to BARKER he laughingly replies)

CECIL
'Excellent news,... do you have the formal papers for Her Majesty to examine'?

(WALSINGHAM is handed the papers by BARKER and as he is handing them to CECIL, nervously says)

WALSINGHAM
'These are the result of many years hard work to condemn the Scottish Queen,... now all we require is...

...the formal signature and grant... for the death warrant... from our gracious Majesty Queen Elizabeth'

(CECIL is overjoyed and retorts)

CECIL

'Her Majesty's signature is but a formality... I have an audience with her today and you can be with me... and you shall have the honour of reading the result to her....
....Thank you Mr BARKER that will be all.....

(BARKER bows slightly and walks out the room)

(After he had left CECIL then says to WALSINGHAM tactfully)

CECIL
'Be so kind as to join me for lunch... I will go to see Her Majesty now to arrange for a formal meeting in the afternoon'

CURTAIN
End of Scene 7

Scene 8

Set in the large throne room with ELIZABETH sitting on her throne dressed in very elaborate dress with many strings of pearls round her neck her red hair visible under a small bonnet.

CECIL and WALSINGHAM are waiting in the room.

ELIZABETH enters from a door in the centre accompanied by several Pages.

Several guards around the room jump to attention.
ELIZABETH walks slowly to the throne and walks up a few steps, turns round and greets CECIL and WALSINGHAM, before sitting on the throne. She says)

ELIZABETH
'Good afternoon Baron Burghley... and Sir Francis,... I trust you are here to bring me tidings from the Star Chamber... on the outcome of the verdict with the trial of Mary Stuart?.

(CECIL looks sheepish but forces a grin)

CECIL
'Yes your Royal Highness.... we have the verdict from the councillors at the Star Chamber....

...It is quite a lengthy document...the verdict of this treasonable act against your presence and safety....

...With your Majesty's permission Sir Francis Walsingham will read the document to you'.

(ELIZABETH waves her hand with a flourish sat on her throne and says softly)

ELIZABETH
'Please continue Gentlemen'.

(WALSINGHAM takes the letter from CECIL and starts to read, slowly and very calmly)

WALSINGHAM
.... 'Thank you your most Gracious Majesty and Baron Burghley.... these are the findings of the Parliament of our noble Lords at your Majesty's Star Chamber.....

.....May it please your most excellent Majesty, our most Gracious Sovereign,... we your humble,... loving and faithful subjects, the Lords and Commons in this present Parliament assembled,... having of long time to our intolerable grief seen by how manifold most...

...dangerous and execrable practices,... ...Mary the daughter and heir of James V , late king of Scots,... dowager of France,... and commonly called Queen of Scots,... hath compassed the Destruction of your majesty's sacred and most royal person,... in whose safety...

...(next under God)... our chief and only felicity doth consist;... and thereby not only to bereave us of the sincere and true Religion of Almighty God,...

...Bringing us and this noble crown back again into the thraldom of the Romish tyranny,... but also utterly to ruinate and overthrow the happy State and Commonweal of this most noble realm;...

...which being from time to time by the great mercy and providence of God, and your Highness's singular wisdom, foreseen and prevented,... your Majesty of your exceeding great clemency and princely magnanimity hath either most graciously passed over, or with singular favour tolerated,... although often and instantly moved by your most loving and faithful subjects to the contrary, in times of your Parliaments, and at many other times;...

....And hath also protected and defended the said Scottish queen.... from those great dangers which her own people,... for certain detestable crimes and offenses to her imputed, had determined against her:
...

...All which notwithstanding,... the same queen was nothing moved with these and many other your Majesty's most gracious favours towards her;...

...But rather obdurate in malice,... and by hope of continual impunity imboldened to prosecute her cruel and mischievous determination by some speedy and violent course;...

....And now lately a very dangerous Plot being conceived and set down by Anthony Babington and others,

(ELIZABETH interrupts and says irritably)

ELIZABETH
' What happened with the estates and properties of Babington and his accomplishes'?

(CECIL answers her)

CECIL
'Your Majesty some few days after, the findings against the accused Mary Stuart a Parliament was holden at Westminster,... begun by virtue of a certain power of vice-gerency,... granted by the Queen to the Arch-bishop of Canterbury,... the Lord Treasurer,... and the Earl of Derby, and that not without precedent. ...

In which Parliament the Proscription of the lord Paget,... Charles Paget,...Sir Francis Englefield,...

...Francis Throckmorton,... Anthony Babington,... Thomas Salisbury,... Edward Jones,... Chidiock Titchbourne,... Charles Tilney,.. and the rest of the Conspirators,... was confirmed,... and their goods and possessions confiscate....

...The estates also of the realm,... which had by their voices approved and confirmed the Sentence given against the Queen of Scots,... did with joint assent put up a Supplication to the Queen by the hands of the Lord Chancellor.'...

(ELIZABETH replies with caustic sarcasm)

ELIZABETH
' Ah-ha....Very good,... these funds from their confiscated possessions will pay for the trials and expense of this

turmoil to England.....
...Please continue Sir Francis.....(She waved her hand with a flourish)

(WALSINGHAM starts to read the document)

WALSINGHAM
'Thank you Your Majesty.....

......That six desperate and wicked persons should undertake that wicked and most horrible enterprise,... to take away your Majesty's life,...

...(whom God of his infinite mercy long preserve)... she did not only give her advice and direction upon every point, and all circumstances concerning the same,.. make earnest request to have it performed with all diligence, but did also promise assurance of large reward and recompense to the doers thereof;...

...Which being informed to your majesty, it pleased your highness,... upon the earnest suit of such as tendered the safety of your royal person,... and the good and quiet state of this realm, to direct your Commission under the great seal of England,...

...To the Lords and others of your Highness's Privy Council,... and certain other Lords of Parliament of the greatest and most ancient degree,... with some of ...your principal judges,... to examine, hear and determine the same cause, and thereupon to give Sentence of Judgment... according to a statute in that behalf, made in the 27th year of your most gracious reign:...

By virtue whereof,... the more part of the same Commissioners, being in number 36,... having at sundry times fully heard what was alleged and proved against the said Scottish queen... in her own presence, touching the said Crimes and Offenses,...

...and what she could say for her Defense and Excuse therein, did after long deliberation give their Sentence and judgment with one consent, that the Death and Destruction... of your royal person was imagined and compassed by the said Anthony Babington,.. with the privity of the same Scottish queen:... and that she herself did also compass and imagine the death and destruction of your most royal person.'...

(ELIZABETH speaks out aggressively)

ELIZABETH
'No prince herein, I confess,... can be silver tied or faster bound than I am with the link of your good will....

....I have had good experience and trial of this world...I know what it is to be a subject, what to be a sovereign, what to have good neighbours,... and sometimes meet evil willers.

...I have found treason in trust, seen great benefits little regarded.

What will my enemies not say,... that for the safety of her life a maiden queen could be content to spill the blood even of her own kinswoman'? ...

(She then signaled to one of her Pages who was standing nearby to come to her she told him)

ELIZABETH
'Bring some refreshments and drinks to Baron Burghley and Sir Francis.... Please continue Sir Francis'

(The Page goes out of the room)

(WALSINGHAM replies politely)

WALSINGHAM
'Thank you Your Majesty and Lord Burghley......where was I?.... Ah yes here we are...

......Now for as much as we your majesty's most humble, loyal and dutiful subjects,....
...representing unto your most Excellent Majesty the universal state of your whole people of all degrees in
this your realm,... do well perceive, and are fully satisfied, that the same Sentence and Judgment is in all things most honourable, just and lawful;...

....And having carefully and effectually,...... according to our most bounden duties, weighed and considered

upon what ground and cause so many
traitorous complots,......
......and dangerous practices against

...your most royal person and estate,...
and for the invading of this realm, have
for the space of many years past grown and
proceeded,... do certainly find, and are
undoubtedly persuaded that all the same
have been from time to time attempted and
practised,.. by and from the Scottish
queen,... and by her confederates,
ministers and favourers,...

...Who conceive an assured hope to achieve
speedily by your Majesty's untimely
death... that which they have long
expected, and whereof during your life....

(WALSINGHAM pauses and looks up at
ELIZABETH, then continues)......

....(which God long preserve to our
inestimable comfort)... they despair; to
wit, to place her the said Scottish
queen... in the imperial and kingly seat
of this realm,... and by her to banish and
destroy the professors and professing of
the true Religion of Jesus Christ..., and
the ancient nobility of this land'....

(ELIZABETH retorts haughtily)

ELIZABETH

'There is one thing higher than

Royalty:... and that is religion,... which causes us to leave the world, and seek God'....

(The Page is standing by the door with a servant with a tray of cups and a beaker with drinks. ELIZABETH motions to them to bring the drinks and a small table beside CECIL and WALSINGHAM.

The servant pours some liquid into the cups for CECIL and WALSINGHAM, both been standing all through the proceedings, both of them take a few sips from the cups, the servant goes away and the Page back to near the side of ELIZABETH.

(She then tells WALSINGHAM)

ELIZABETH
'Please carry on Sir Francis'

(Walsingham puts his cup down on the table, gives a little cough and says)

WALSINGHAM
'Thank you your Majesty for the drink I was getting a little thirsty.....If I may read on your Majesty and Lord Burghley.......here we are.....

.......and to bring this whole state and commonweal to foreign subjection, and utter ruin and confusion:..

...Which their malicious and traitorous

purpose they will never cease to prosecute by all possible means they can,.... so long as they may have their eyes and imaginations fixed upon that Lady,... the only ground of their treasonable hope and conceits, and the only seed-plot of all dangerous and traitorous devices and practices against your sacred person.....

...And seeing also what insolent boldness is grown in the heart of the same queen,... through your Majesty's former exceeding favours and clemencies towards her;... and thereupon weighing with heavy and sorrowful hearts, in what continual peril of such like desperate conspiracies and practices your majesty's most royal and sacred person and life....

....(more dear unto us than our own)... is and shall be still, without any possible means to prevent it, so long as the Scottish queen... shall be suffered to continue, and shall not receive that due punishment,

….which by justice, and the laws of this your realm,... she hath so often and so many ways for her most wicked and detestable offences deserved:

Therefore,... and for that we find, that if the said lady should now escape the due and deserved punishment of Death....
....for these her most execrable- Treasons

and Offences, your highnesses royal person shall be exposed unto many more, and those more secret and dangerous Conspiracies than before.'...

(ELIZABETH intervenes, she is fidgeting irritably and says)

ELIZABETH

'My mortal foe... can no ways wish me a greater harm than England's hate;... neither should death be less welcome unto me than such a mishap betide me....

....Please continue Sir Francis'....

(WALSINGHAM looks sheepishly at her and starts to read)

WALSINGHAM

'And such as shall not or cannot be foreseen, or discovered, as these late attempts have been;....
.... and shall not hereafter beso well able to remove or take away the ground and occasion of the same, as now by justice may or ought to be done:...

....We do most humbly beseech your most Excellent Majesty,... that as well in respect of the continuance of the true religion now professed amongst us,... and of the safety of your most royal person and estate, as in regard of the preservation and defence of us your most loving,... dutiful and faithful subjects, and the whole commonweal of this realm;...

It may please your Highness to take speedy order, That declaration of the same sentence and judgment be made

...and published by proclamation,.... and that thereupon direction be given for further proceedings against the said Scottish queen,... according to the effect and true meaning of the said statute:

(ELIZABETH exclaims simply and proudly)

ELIZABETH

....'God has given such brave soldiers to this Crown that,... if they do not frighten our neighbours,... at least they prevent us from being frightened by them....
....Are you almost finished Sir Francis?...

....Carry on Sir...

(WALSINGHAM replies without looking at her)

WALSINGHAM

....'Thank you your Majesty. ....

....Yes I am at the last page only a few passages to read,... if I may your majesty and Lord Burghley......

..........Because upon advised and great consultation, we cannot find that there is any possible means to provide for your Majesty's safety, but by the just and speedy execution of the said queen,... the neglecting ...whereof may procure the heavy
displeasure and punishment of Almighty God,... as by sundry severe examples of his great justice in that behalf left us in the sacred scriptures doth appear....

....And if the same be not put in present execution,... we your most loving and dutiful subjects shall thereby

...(so far as man's reason can reach)... be brought into utter despair of the continuance amongst us of the true religion of Almighty God,... and of your Majesty's life,... and the safety of all your faithful subjects, and the good estate of this most flourishing commonweal.'...

.....'This is the end of the documents Your Majesty'...

(He hands the documents to CECIL who starts

to speak)

>CECIL
>....'Thank you your majesty for your patience and understanding.....

.....Thank you Sir Francis for delivering this serious historical document.....

....Your Gracious Majesty I will leave this document for your examination and reply.

(CECIL nods to the Page who comes over and takes the documents from CECIL....

....Then he speaks to ELIZABETH)

>CECIL
>....'Thank you your Majesty, I beg now to take your leave with Sir Francis'

(ELIZABETH is handed the documents by her Page. She glances at the 1st page. Looks towards Cecil and with a reproachful look says)

>ELIZABETH
>' Thank you Baron Burghley and Sir Francis.....(She pauses)...

(She continues)...
.......'Your judgment I condemn not, neither do I mistake your reasons, but pray you to accept my thankfulness,... excuse my doubtfulness,... and take in good part my answer, answer-less......(She pauses

again to gather her thoughts).......

' I will have my reply on the morrow... and would like to confirm that you can be here...

....I will also summon the Earl of Shrewsbury... with the Earl of Kent and Robert Beale the Clerk of the Council to be here......(She pauses, raises her voice and her hand).......
.......'Those who touch the scepters of princes deserve no pity'.......

...'That will be all gentlemen I will see you on the morrow'....

(CECIL and WALSINGHAM bow deeply and move backwards to the exit door and leave the room)

(CURTAIN)

END OF SCENE 8

SCENE 9

The Throne room;

The Lords are assembled CECIL, WALSINGHAM, Earl of SHREWSBURY, Earl of KENT, ROBERT BEALE and DAVISON the Secretary of ELIZABETH.

All the Lords are standing as no-one could sit in the presence of the monarch when dealing with a serious matter of The State.

They have to stand during all the procedure...

There is a table set with drinks and some fruit near the wall of the room, with 2 servants standing by.

(ELIZABETH enters into the room with her Pages behind her, she walks up the steps to the throne,
acknowledging the gathering,.... fussing with her bulky dress, she sits on the throne, then announces)...

ELIZABETH

'Greetings my Lords and Gentlemen.....thank you for your attendance on this grim subject....that is without doubt one of the greatest tragedy's of my life to discuss....

...My secretary Mr DAVISON will read my reply to the documents presented on the outcome of the trial... and decisions reached about Mary Stuart... in the Star

Chamber of my Parliament....

...I had intended to read my reply myself, however... I find the proceedings very emotional....

(She makes a slight cough).....

....Therefore my secretary will read my reply on my behalf......
.....Please start Mr DAVISON....

(DAVISON walks to the side of the throne he has the documents in his hands, straightening his shoulders, concealing a feeling of shame he announces loud and clear)

DAVISON
.....'In the name of Our Gracious Majesty Queen ELIZABETH...Queen of England,.. Ireland and France.....
....I am instructed by Our Gracious Majesty to read her honourable reply to my Lords and Gentlemen before us today......

...(DAVISON turns and looks at Elizabeth, she waves her hand softly and nods to him. He looks at the assembly then holds the document straight out in front of him at eye level then reads out clearly)...........

DAVISON .....

" So many and so great are the bottomless graces,.... and immeasurable benefits bestowed upon me by the Almighty.... that I must not only most humbly acknowledge them as benefits,.... but admire them as miracles,... being in no sort able to express them.....

.....And though there liveth not any that may more justly acknowledge himself bound to God than I... whose life he hath miraculously preserved from so many dangers,...... yet am I not more deeply bound to give him thanks for any one thing,... than for this which I will now tell you,... and which I account as a miracle:

....Namely,..... that as I came to the crown with the most hearty good-will of all my subjects,.... so now after 28 years reign,... I perceive in them the same,... if not greater good- will towards me;... which if I once lose,... well might I breathe,... ..but never think I lived...

(ELIZABETH coughs gently, DAVISON turns to look at her as this was her signal when she wants to speak...she says.... darkly)....

ELIZABETH

....'I have this day been in greater conflict with myself,.... than ever in all my life,... whether I should speak,... or hold my peace....

......If I speak and not complain,.... I shall dissemble:....... and if I should be silent your labour taken were all in vain...

.......If I should complain,... it might seem strange and rare;..... yet I confess that my most hearty desire was,....... that some other means might have been devised to work your security and my safety,.... than this which is now propounded...

......So as I cannot but complain,..... though not of
you... yet unto you;.... that I perceive by your petitions,(Her voice and eyes raised).... that my safety dependeth wholly upon the death of another...
........Carry on Mr DAVISON.....

(DAVISON looks at ELIZABETH and quickly replies)...

DAVISON
...'Certainly your majesty, thank you your majesty....
Your majesty and my Lords the reply of Our Gracious Majesty Queen ELIZABETH.....

(He pauses and raises the document to eye level coughs, and begin reading again).....

.....And now though my life hath been dangerously shot at,.... yet I protest there is nothing hath more grieved me,..... than that one not differing from me in sex,.. of like rank and degree,... of the same stock,... and most nearly allied unto me in blood,... hath fallen into so great a crime. ...

.....And so far have I been from bearing her any ill-will,.. that upon the discovery of certain treason-able practices against me,...I wrote unto her secretly,.. that if she would confess them by a private letter unto myself, ..they should be wrapped up in silence. ...

...Neither did I write thus in mind to entrap her,... for I knew then as much as she could confess...

...And even yet,... though the matter become thus far,... if she would truly repent,.. and no man would undertake her cause against me,.... and if my life alone depended hereupon,.... and not the safety and welfare of my whole people, I would......... (I protest

unfeignedly)....most willingly pardon
her....

...Nay if England might by my death attain
a more flourishing estate,... and a better
prince,... I would most gladly lay down my
life:...

..For, for your sakes it is, and for my
people's, that I desire to live...

.....As for me,... I see no such great
cause why I should either be fond to
live,.. or fear to die...
I have had good experience of this world,
and I know what it is to be a subject, and
what to be a sovereign.....

.....Good neighbours I have had,.. and I
have met with bad;.. and in trust I have
found treason. I have bestowed benefits
upon ill deserver's; and where I have done
well, have been ill requited.....

(DAVISON stops and sips some water and at
this point ELIZABETH tells the assembled
Lords who are all standing in the presence
of the queen to have some refreshment)...

ELIZABETH......
'Gentlemen... please help yourselves to
some refreshments on the table over
there... (She points at a table by the
wall)

(Here follows a long discourse on the danger to the Queen's life and the established religion, with a statement that all England asked the speedy execution of Mary, late Queen of Scots).

(After they have finished and move back to their places before ELIZABETH, CECIL takes the initiative to say something he speaks defensively aggressive)......

CECIL

....'Your Majesty.... my fellow Lords and the whole Realm of England are desperately worried for your safety as long as Mary Stuart is alive...I must be emphatic as to how dangerous this woman is to you and England.....she has been found guilty of treasonable acts....and I must remind you that she claims to be the True and only Queen of England....

(Pause, he looks at WALSINGHAM and around at the others standing next to him, they all murmur and nod in agreement. He turns to ELIZABETH and speaks in a fuming manner)....

CECIL
...'I must remind Your Majesty that the Scottish Queen was also guilty of bearing

the Arms of England on her shield...

....And she claimed that her father-in law Henri Deux of France.... had commanded her to carry the Arms of England,... even after she had left France and returned to Scotland.

(Pause...a few grumbles around him, he goes on).....

CECIL
...' She claimed to me when I challenged her....that she had no intentions of denying her rights.....

(ELIZABETH ....toying with her pearls and looking agitated...speaks sharply)......

ELIZABETH
...'If there be any that think I have ....prolonged the time of purpose to make a counterfeit shew of clemency,... they do me the most undeserved wrong,... as He knoweth, which is the searcher of the most secret thoughts of the heart. ....

Or,.... if there be any that be persuaded,..... that the commissioners durst not pronounce other sentence,..... as fearing thereby to displease me,... or to seem to fail of their care for my safety,...
they but heap upon me most injurious

conceits.

For either those,... whom I have put in trust,.... have failed of their duties or else they signified unto the commissioners in my name,... that my will and pleasure...

...was,... that every one should deal freely according to his conscience,..and what they would not openly

declare,... that they should reveal unto me in private....

....It was of my most favourable mind towards her,... that I desired some other means might be found out to prevent this mischief.....

.....But since now it is resolved,.... that my surety is,.... most desperate without her
death,... I have a most inward feeling of sorrow,.... that I,... which have in my time pardoned so many rebels,... winked at so many treasons,... or neglected them with silence;.... must now seem to shew cruelty upon so great a princess.... I have,... since I came to the crown of this realm,... seen many defamatory Books and Pamphlets against me..... accusing me to be a tyrant;..
.. well fare the writers hearts,... I believe their meaning was to tell me news:.... and news indeed it was to me,...

to be branded with the note of tyranny :

(She then speaks to DAVISON)

'Mr DAVISON please continue reading my statement'...

(DAVISON turns to her and bows and lifts the letter and says)....

DAVISON

.....'Thank you Your Majesty, this is where I stopped,.... may I point out that copies of these documents will be given to everyone here and sent to all the Realm of England....Her Majesty's reply if I may continue, she said.......

.....While I call to mind these things past,... behold things present,.. and expect things to come,.. I hold them happiest that go hence soonest......

......Nevertheless against such mischiefs as these,.. I put on a better courage than is common to my sex,... so as whatsoever befall me,.. death shall not take me unprepared. ...

.......And as touching these Treasons,.... I will not so prejudicate myself,.. or the laws of my kingdom,.. as not but to think that she having been the contriver of the same treasons,.. was bound and liable to the ancient laws,... though the late act had never been made;

which notwithstanding was no ways made to prejudice her......

......So far was it from being made to entrap her,.. that it was rather intended to forewarn and terrify her from attempting anything against it.......

But seeing it was now in force of a law,.... I thought good to proceed against her according to the same.

..But you lawyers are so curious in scanning the nice points of the law,.... and following of precedents and form,.. rather than expounding the laws themselves,... that by exact observing of your form,.. she must have been indicted in Staffordshire,.... and have holden up her hand at the bar,... and have been tried by a jury of twelve men...

...A proper course forsooth of trial against a princess!...

To avoid therefore such absurdities,... I thought it better to refer the examination of so weighty a cause to a good number of the noblest personages of the land,... and the judges of the realm;.... and all little enough....

For we princes are set as it were upon stages,.. in the sight and view of all the world....

(ELIZABETH coughs gently to signal to DAVISON that she wants to speak...worriedly impressed by DAVISON delivery she interrupts him saying)....

ELIZABETH
....'I would it were as great news to hear of their

impiety. ...

...But what is it which they will not write now,.... when they shall hear that I have given consent,.... that the executioner's hands shall be imbrued in the blood of my nearest kinswoman?...

....But so far am I from cruelty,.... that to save mine own life,... I would not offer her violence;.... neither have I been so careful how to prolong mine own life,..... as how to preserve both:... which that it is now impossible,... I grieve exceedingly.

....I am not so void of judgment,..... as not to see mine own perils before mine eyes;.... nor so mad,....

(Pause- then with despairing pessimism).... to sharpen a sword to cut mine own throat;

(Pause- angry-)..... nor so careless,.... as not to provide for the safety of mine own life.

....But this I consider with myself,.... that man,.... a man would put his own life in danger to save a princess's life....

I do not say,..... so will I;..... yet have I many times thought upon it......

But seeing so many have both written and spoken against me,
(Pause-disgustedly)..... give me leave,.... I pray you,

(Pause-pleading)..... to say somewhat in mine own defense,... that ye may see what manner of woman I am,..... for whose safety you have passed such careful thoughts;....
.....wherein as I do with most thankful heart consider your vigilant care,.... so am I sure I shall never requite it,... had I as many lives as you all........

(ELIZABETH stops here and dries her eyes with her...
...handkerchief...DAVISON.... calls out)....

DAVISON
.....'Your Majesty... are you well enough to continue with this very troublesome'....

(ELIZABETH ...sobbing gently coughs out)
.....

ELIZABETH
...'Yes DAVISON I am alright but very distressed in what we have to do,... please carry on reading the documents'.....

(DAVISON replies)....

....'Thank you Your Majesty I am almost finished.... Your Majesty and my Lords please if I may.....

(He lifts the letter to eye level and reads out loud, but a little more quickly).....

DAVISON
....'The least spot is soon spied in our garments,... a blemish quickly noted in our doings....

...It behoveth us therefore to be careful that our proceedings be just and honourable....

But I must tell you one thing,.... that by this last act of parliament you have brought me to a narrow straight,.. that I must give order for her death... which is a princess most nearly allied unto me in blood,..... and whose practices against me have stricken me into so great grief,.... that I have been glad to absent myself from this parliament,... lest I should increase my sorrow by hearing it spoken of, and not out of fear of any danger,.... as some think...

(ELIZABETH stands up then swoons back onto her throne...DAVISON rushes up to her aid...the other Lords also come to her side...everyone was in a flurry...CECIL calls to the PAGE)...

CECIL

'Bring some water quickly'...

(The PAGE goes to the table with the refreshments and fills a goblet, then brings it to CECIL, he gives ELIZABETH a sip)

CECIL

'Your Majesty...you are very distressed may I suggest we end this session...we can continue another day and we have copies of your statements to bring to the Parliament'...

(Elizabeth nods her approval she is helped by DAVISON and CECIL from the throne and through her private door)

(CECIL with WALSINGHAM and the other Lords in the throne room)

CECIL

'Her Majesty is too un-well to continue...we must carry on and get the death warrant drawn up to eradicate the problem of Mary Stuart...this will take a few months as we have got to make sure that France and Spain will not intervene...We must brief all our Ambassadors to set up a propaganda against Mary Stuart...with the results of the court findings and the Parliament verdict...but we have to keep secret the trial details...so make sure that all the councillors are informed to say nothing about the trial'...

WALSINGHAM

'But surely Mary Stuart and her people who were at the trial will tell people of who we fixed it'...

CECIL

'Don't worry about that as we can deny everything they say...Right Gentlemen...lets get the wheels in motion'

(CURTAIN)

END OF SCENE 9

SCENE 10

(In the luxurious private office of ELIZABETH sitting at her desk...Opposite were CECIL, WALSINGHAM, EARL OF KENT, EARL OF SHREWSBURY and DAVISON everyone was darkly serious. CECIL starts talking)

CECIL

'Your Majesty...the death sentence was pronounced and verified by the Lords in the Parliament... Lord Buckhurst and Beale have been sent to the queen of Scots,... to signify unto that Sentence was pronounced against her;..
...that the same was approved and confirmed by act of parliament,... as most just,... and the Execution thereof instantly sued for by the Estates, out of a due regard of justice,... security and necessity:

...and therefore to persuade her to acknowledge her Of-
fences against God and Your Majesty... and to expiate them before her death by repentance:...
letting her understand, that as long as she lived, the received Religion in England could not subsist.

....That she was holden to be an instrument

for the re-establishing of the Roman Catholic Religion in this island.
> Elizabeth (Frowning)

'What was her reply'?

CECIL

'She prayed, that she might have a Catholic priest to direct her conscience, and minister the Sacraments unto her....

She was offered a bishop and a dean whom they commended unto her for this use, she utterly rejected this suggestion, and sharply taxed the English nation, saying... often.... That the English had many times slaughtered their kings; no marvel therefore, if they now also shew their cruelty upon me, that am issued from the blood of their kings...

...I have the death warrant for Your Majesty to sign'...
(ELIZABETH to DAVISON)

ELIZABETH

'Mr. DAVISON bring me a pen and ink...

(She reads out part of the warrant)

ELIZABETH

" Elizabeth, by the grace of God, queen of

England,
France and Ireland.

To our trusty and well-beloved cousins, George Earl of Shrewsbury, Earl marshal of England;

Henry Earl of Kent; Henry Earl of Derby;

George Earl of Cumberland; and Henry Earl of Pembroke, greeting.

Whereas sit-hence the Sentence given by you, and others of our council,... nobility and judges,... against the queen of Scots,... by the name of Mary,... the daughter of James V., late king of Scots, commonly called the queen of Scots, and dowager of France,.. as to you is well known;

all the States in the last Parliament assembled, did not only deliberately, by great advice... allow and approve the same Sentence as just and honourable, but also with all humbleness and earnestness possible, at sundry times require, solicit, and press us to direct such further Execution against her person, as they did adjudge her to have daily deserved....

I do authorize you,... as soon as you shall have time convenient,... to repair to our Castle of Fotheringay,... where the said queen of Scots is in custody of our right trusty and faithful servant and counsellor, sir Amias Powlet.

...Then taking her into your charge, to cause by your commandment Execution to be done upon her
person,... in the presence of yourselves, and the aforesaid Sir Amias Powlet.

...And of such other officers of justice as you shall command to attend upon you for that purpose; and the same to be done in such manner and form, and at such time and place,... and by such persons, as to five, four or three of you, shall be thought by your discretions convenient... notwithstanding any law, statute or ordinance to the contrary.

And these our letters patent sealed with our great seal of England,... shall be to you, and every of you, and to all persons that shall be present, or that shall be, by you,... commanded to do any thing appertaining to the aforesaid Execution...

A full sufficient Warrant, and Discharge forever.

And further, we are also pleased and contented, and hereby we do will, command and authorize our Chancellor of England,... at the requests of you all, and every of you, that the duplicate of our

Letters Patent, be to all purposes made, dated and sealed with our great Seal of England,... as these presents now are:...

In witness whereof, we have caused these our letters to be made patent....

...At our manor of Greenwich,... the 1st day of February,1587... in the 29th year of our reign."

DAVISON...Give me the quill....

....Signed ELIZABETH R...

...Very well, my Lords you have the warrant see that it is implemented as soon as possible'...

(ELIZABETH hands the document to CECIL)

CECIL

'Thank you Your Majesty...we will make haste...now I beg your pardon to make leave of your presence with my Lords....

ELIZABETH

'Thank you my Lords...go and do what you have to do'...

(CECIL and the Lords back out of the door)

(CURTAIN)

END OF SCENE 10

SCENE 11

7th February 1587-Fotheringay Castle.

(Hereupon without any delay Beale, who in respect of religion was the queen of Scots most bitter adversary, was sent down with one or two Executioners, and a Warrant, wherein authority was given to the Earls of Shrewsbury, Kent, Derby, Cumberland, and others, to
see Execution done according to law;

As soon as the Earls arrive at Fotheringay, they, together with sir Amias Powlet, and sir Drew Drury, to
whose custody the queen of Scots was committed, came to her at her bare prison cell, and told her the cause of their coming, reading the Death Warrant, and in few words admonished her to prepare herself for Death, for she was to die the next day).

EARL OF KENT

'Madam..I have been ordered by our Gracious Majesty Queen ELIZABETH...to bring forth to you this order that you are to be executed tomorrow morning at 8 o'clock.

I am here with witnesses, The EARL OF SHREWSBURY... The EARL OF DERBY... The EARL OF CUMBERLAND...I am The EARL OF KENT...and in the company of Sir AMIAS POWLET and Sir DREW DRURY.

This is a copy of the Death Warrant...have you anything to say?...

(KENT hands MARY the letter...she looks at it briefly and puts it on the table. She undauntedly, and with a composed spirit, Answers);

MARY

"I did not think the queen,... my sister,... would have consented to my death,...as I... who am not subject to your law and jurisdiction:... but seeing her pleasure is so....

I am thankful such welcome news...You do me great good in withdrawing me from this world out of which I am glad to go, on account of the miseries I see in it and of being myself in continual affliction...

I have expected this for eighteen years...

...I am a Queen born and a Queen anointed, the near relation of the Queen of England and great grand-daughter to Henry VII King of England;...and I have had the honour to be Queen of France...

...Yet throughout my life I have experienced great misfortune and now I am glad that it has pleased God by means of you to take me away from so many troubles...

I am ready and willing to shed my blood in the cause of God my Saviour and Creator and the Catholic Church, for the maintenance of which I have always done everything within my power.

...Death shall be to me most welcome;... neither is that soul worthy of the high and everlasting joys above, whose body cannot endure one stroke of the executioner....

I would like me to be comforted by my priest
and confessor to make my last confession
and have absolution... before I die... and
my Master of my Household... Mr.
Melvin'...

(MARY lifts her Bible from the table she
kisses her Bible then speaks softly)

MARY
'I have never desired the death of the
Queen of England nor endeavoured to bring
it about, nor that of any other person.'

(KENT Angry and vicious looking scornfully
at MARY'S Bible)

KENT (Sternly savage)
'As that is a Popish Testament you hold,
an oath taken on it is worthless...You will
not be allowed to have a Catholic Priest
for any purpose...this is strictly
forbidden...however...you can have the
comfort and services of our Bishop...or
the dean of Peterborough, to comfort you'

MARY (Softly)

'Mine is the true Testament in my
opinion...Would you prefer me to swear on
your version in which I do not believe...

I have long lived in the true Faith...
...I shall not change now.

...I require not your Bishop or your dean of Peterborough...as I do not conform to your faith or their faiths...as I am a Roman Catholic and this is the only faith I live for and will die for...as God is my witness'...

(The earl of Kent, in a hot burning zeal to religion, breaks forth into these words among other speeches:

KENT (Raging and ranting)

" Your life will be the death of our Religion,... as contrariwise your death... will be the life thereof of the English Religion....you collaborated with traitors
Anthony Babington and others..."

MARY

'The Mention being made of Babington, this I constantly deny...and his Conspiracy to have been at all known to me, and the revenge of my wrong I leave to God....

...What was become of my secretaries Naw and Curle;   has it ever been heard of before, that servants were suborned and accepted as Witnesses against their master's life?...

KENT (Waiving his hand dismissing

MARY)

'Madam... it is not of my interest to talk of your secretaries...I am here for one purpose...along with these other gentlemen...and to make sure our duties are carried out on the morrow...come now Gentlemen we must retire to another place to make sure everything is in order...for this woman's executioner'...

(MARY turns to SHREWSBURY and asks him)

MARY

'At what hour am I to die?'

(SHREWSBURY Lowering his eyes, his voice trembling as he speaks)

SHREWSBURY

'Tomorrow morning at eight o'clock.'

MARY

'There is little time left to me...Go now and leave me in peace.'

(The earls then depart, MARY asks her friends Jane Kennedy and Elizabeth Curle for supper to be hastened, that she might the better dispose of her concerns.)

MARY
'Dearest Jane and Elizabeth could you

arrange for supper to be brought soon...

And be so kind to ask Sir Andrew Melville and my physician Doctor Bourgoigne and my surgeon Doctor Gourion and my apothecary Doctor Gervais to join us'?

(Jane Kennedy, Elizabeth Curle, Andrew Melville, Doctor Bourgoigne, Doctor Gourion and Doctor Gervais all join MARY for their last supper together in her tiny room.

They are all terribly distressed.

She sups temperately, as her manner is; and seeing her servants, both men and women, weeping and lamenting as she sits at supper, she comforts them
with great courage and magnanimity, bade them leave mourning, and rather rejoice, that she was now to
depart out of a world of miseries.

MARY
'Please do not weep and cry for me as now I will join my Sweet Lord Jesus...who will comfort me in my new home with him...

My dearest friends now you must rejoice and share in my happiness that I am about to leave this world that has brought me so much misery and unhappiness'...

(Everyone starts to wail and cry very loudly)

(Turning to Bourgoingne, her physician, she asks him)

MARY
'Doctor Bourgoingne... do you not now find the force of Truth to be great'...

(Bourgoingne could only nod in agreement as he is choked with emotion)

MARY (With great strength)

" They say,... that I must die,... because I have plotted against the queen's life;... yet the Earl of Kent tells me,... there is no other cause of my death, but that they are afraid for their Religion because of me;...

I will die in the truth of my Roman Catholique faith the only true faith of Jesus Christ in the manner of the martyred Saints before me....

The Apostles of my dear sweet Lord Jesus...

Peter; James; John; Andrew; Philip; Matthew; Thomas; James, the son of Alpheus; Bartholomew; Judas Thaddeus; and Simon Zelotes; Paul; Perpetula; Felicity; Patrick; Columba; Ninian; Augustine; Eanswithe; Bede; Cuthbert; Wilfred.

I am Mary Madeleine.

Neither hath my offence against the queen,... but their fear because of me,... drawn this end upon me, while some,... under the colour of Religion,.. and the public good, aim at their own private respects and advantages....come now we must sit together and eat our last supper together..."

(Towards the end of supper she raises her glass to all her servants and friends)

MARY

'Now I propose a toast to each and everyone of you for the love and care and devotion you have shown to me.'

(Her friends all knell before her pledged her in order upon their knees, mingling tears with the wine, and begging pardon for their neglect of their duty ; as she also in like manner does of them).

MARY

'After supper I will peruse my Will, read over the Inventory of my Goods and Jewels, and write down the Names of those, to whom I bequeath every
particular I have'.

(No-one could speak...To some she distributes money with her own hand).

Mary

'Now if you can allow me a little time to write some letters...

I will write to my Confessor, that he would make intercession for me to God in his prayers....

And also letters of recommendation for yourselves to the French King and the Duke of Guise.

And ask for safe passage for yourselves...after I have been taken to my Lord Jesus'...

(They all leave her room and she sits at her table writing)

(MARY speaking as she is writing to her French brother-in-law)

MARY (Writing and speaking)

..*'Today, after dinner I was advised of my sentence.*

I am to be executed like a criminal at eight o' clock in the morning.

I haven't had enough time to give you a full account of all that has happened, but if you will listen to my physician and my other sorrowful servants, you will know the truth, and how, thanks be to God, I scorn death and faithfully protest that I face it innocent of any crime....

The Catholic faith and the defence of my God-giver right to the English throne are the two reasons for which I am condemned, and yet they will not allow me to say that it is for the Catholic faith that I die...

I beg you as Most Christian Majesty, my brother-in-law and old friend, who have always protested your love for me, to give proof now of your kindness on all these points : both by paying charitably my unfortunate servants their arrears of wages
(this is a burden on my conscience that you alone can relieve), and also by having prayers offered to God for a Queen who has herself been called Most Christian, and who dies a Catholic, stripped of all her possessions..

Concerning my son, I commend him to you inasmuch as he deserves it, as I cannot answer for him...
I venture to send you two precious stones, amulets against illness, trusting that you will enjoy good health and a long and happy

life.

Your beloved sister Marie R....

(She kneels down and prays beside her bed then goes to bed, slept some hours; and then waking, with a fright, in the dark room CECIL and WALSINGHAM were standing over her she screams loudly)

CECIL (Sharply to WALSINGHAM)

'Hold her mouth and grab her arms...now you bitch I will show you something'...

(MARY'S little dog is at the foot of her bed and as CECIL tries to lay on top of MARY the little Terrier bites him on the cheek...the dog is barking as CECIL jumps away from... ...MARY...WALSINGHAM lets go of her...

Suddenly the room door bursts open and MARYS friends dash in and start beating the two men with loud screams and oaths... the Captain of the guard also runs in with guards and drag CECIL and WALSINGHAM out... the guards needed no explanation as they push and shove CECIL and WALSINGHAM)

MARY (Crying but calm)

'I'm all right my friends my little baby saved me from shame and from those beasts...now I will pray for the rest of my time'...

Melville
'We will all stay with you and join you in your prayers Your Majesty'...

(They all knell down together and start to pray. Then MARY says)

MARY
'It is now time for me to make myself ready and for you men to leave me until I dress...come now ladies I must prepare myself'...

(The men leave the room)

Mary (Strongly)
'Now ladies I have but a few hours to live...Come, help me dress as for a festival...I want to wear my finest in my kirtle of black satin and my petticoat of crimson velvet...the colour of martyrdom...my pale blue stockings...also the beautiful camisole you made for me...

My friends, do now desert me when I am dead.

When I am no longer able to, see that my body is decently covered'....

(Mary touches the shoulder of JANE KENNEDY who is overcome with emotion)

MARY

'Do not be distressed, Jane...
This has been coming for a long time....Try to welcome it as I do...But I would not wish this poor body to be degraded in death...So make sure I am covered decently'...

(Jane can only nod)

MARY

'Now help me with my black satin widow's gown and Agnus Dei...and my girdle with the cross for round my waist...
You must take care of my poor little dog when I am gone...he does not know that this is our last goodbye between us'...

(ELIZABETH CURLE Stammers)

ELIZABETH

'Have no fear for him, Your Majesty...But I think he will doubtless die of sorrow...as I fear I may'...

MARY

'Nay, you must live and remember this: Your sorrow is greater than mine...So do not mourn for me...You will be released from your prison...Think of that'...

(Both women cannot speak any more and continue to help MARY dress and place a coif and a flowing veil of white gauze on her chestnut hair)

MARY

'There, I am ready now...Dressed as for a festival...

Leave me now for a while...that I may pray for the courage I may need.'

(Both women leave silently out of her room)

(The Earls SHREWSBURY and KENT burst into MARY'S room while MARY is praying)

KENT (With aggression)

'Come forth now it is time to face your Maker'...

(MARY'S friends Jane Kennedy, Elizabeth Curle, Andrew Melville, Doctor Bourgoigne, Doctor Gourion and Doctor Gervais come to her room when they heard the noise)

MARY

'Can my friends and I say a last prayer together?...

KENT

'No...come now'...

(CURTAIN)

SCENE 12

(In the hall with sighs and groans, her friends start to wail)...

And forth she comes with state, into the same great hall she was tried in....she bares great countenance and presence majestically composed; a cheerful look, and a matron-like and modest habit;

her head is covered with a linen veil, and that is hanging down to the ground, her prayer beads hanging at her girdle, and carrying her Crucifix and Bible in her hands. In the porch she is received by the Earls and other noblemen, where Melville, falling upon his knees, and pouring forth tears, bewails.

There is a large stage with two steps leading up to it... in the middle of the hall... and many people standing around the room.

The executioner is standing by the Block that is covered in a black cloth)

   MELVILLE (Crying)

'Woe is me ,that I have to carry into Scotland the woeful tidings of the unhappy fate of my lady
and mistress'...

(She thus comforts him)

   MARY (Solemnly)

"Lament not, but rather rejoice, thou shalt by-and-by see Mary Stuart freed from all her cares.... Tell them,

...that I die constant in my Religion, and firm in my fidelity and affection towards Scotland and France.... God forgive them,... who have thirsted after my blood, as harts do after the fountain!...

Thou, God! who art Truth itself, and perfectly and truly understandest the inward thoughts of my heart, knowest how greatly I have desired that the kingdoms of England and Scotland might be united into one...

….Commend me to my son, and assure him, that I have done nothing, which may be prejudicial to the kingdom of Scotland;... admonish him to hold in amity and friendship with the queen of England;... and
see thou do him faithful service."

(With now the tears trickling down, she bids Melville
several times farewell, who weeps as fast as she. Then
turning to the Earls, she asks them)

MARY (Pleading)

'Please be civil that my friends...that they might enjoy their Legacies, that they may stand by me at my
Death,... and might be sent back into their own country
with letters of safe conduct'....

(The earl of Kent shewed himself somewhat unwilling, fearing some superstition).

KENT (Sharply)
'I am not happy to have them at your death

for fear of some unnatural happening'

MARY (Softly)

" Fear it not... These harmless souls desire only to take their last farewell of me: I know my sister Elizabeth would not have denied me so so small a matter,... that my women should be then present, were it but for the honour of the female sex...

I am her near kinswoman, descended from Henry VII., queen dowager of France, and anointed queen of Scots,"

(When she says and turns herself aside, it was at last granted, that such of her servants as she
should name should be present by nods from SHREWSBURY and KENT).

MARY (Pleading)

'Please allow, Jane Kennedy, Elizabeth Curle, Andrew Melville, Doctor Bourgoigne, Doctor Gourion and Doctor Gervais to be present at my death to witness for the world'...

(So the, two Earls and the sheriff going before her, she comes to the scaffold, which is built at the upper end of the Hall, on which was placed a chair, a cushion, and a block, all covered with black cloth.

As soon as she is set down, and silence commanded, Beale reads the warrant:

She hears it attentively, yet as if her thoughts were taken up with somewhat else.

The room is filled with people and guards.

Then Fletcher, dean of Peterborough, tries to begin a long speech to her touching the Condition of her Lifepast, present, and to come.

She interrupts him as he is speaking)

                    FLETCHER
(Aggressively)

'Madam...you are condemned to death...you must now accept the faith of England...

                 MARY (Saintly)

'Do not trouble yourself my Religion was firmly fixed and resolved in the ancient Catholic Roman Religion, and for it...I am ready to shed my last blood'...

                 FLETCHER (Rudely)

'Madam...come to true repentance, and to put your whole
trust in Christ by an assured faith;'...

(She answers).

MARY (With dignity)

' Sir... in my Catholic Religion I was both born and bred, and I am now ready to die'...

(The Earls ask if they would pray with her; to whom she says)

MARY (Dismissively)

'I would give yourselves hearty thanks, if yourselves would pray for me:... but to join, in prayer with you, who are of another profession, would be in me a heinous sin'.

(Then they appointed the dean to pray; with whom while the multitude that stood round about were praying, she falls down upon her knees and holding the Crucifix before her in her hands, prays in Latin, with her friends)

(After the Dean calls an end of praying)

FLECHER (Viscously)

'Enough of these Popish prayers'

MARY (Solemnly)

'I recommended the church, my son, and queen Elizabeth to God, I beseech God to turn away His wrath from this island, and professing, that I repose my hope of Salvation in the blood of Christ:'

(Lifting up her Crucifix)

MARY (In prayer)

'I call on the Celestial Choir of Saints to
make intercession to God for me:... I forgive all my
enemies...
...O my Lord and my God, I have trusted in Thee... O my dear Jesus, now liberate me... In shackle and chain, in torture and pain, I long for Thee.

...In weakness and sighing, in kneeling and crying, I adore and implore Thee to liberate me...From my tormentors and oppression...

(Kissing the crucifix, and signing herself with the Cross, she says)

MARY (Calling out loud)

"As Thy arms, Christ! were spread out upon the cross, so receive me with the stretched-out arms of Thy mercy, and forgive my sins."

(Then the executioners ask her forgiveness, which she grants them. And when her women are taking off her upper garments which she was eager and hasty to have done, wailing and lamenting the while, she kisses them; and signing them with the Cross, with a cheerful countenance)

MARY (Softly)

'I forgive yourselves...I bid yourselves forbear your lamentations, for now I should rest from all my sorrows... I have no regrets'...

Kent (Shouting Angrily)

'Do You have no regrets...for your life or Popish faith'?

(Mary turns and looks at him and smiles as she gently retorts)

MARY

'Non, je ne regrette rien...

in My End is my Beginning..and my son who is baptized a Roman Catholic will rule this land...when your barren Tudor dynasty is no more'...

(In the same manner turns to her men, who also weep, she signs them with the Cross, and smiling, bids them
farewell. And now having covered her face

with a linen handkerchief, and laying herself down to the block, she recites the Psalm),

MARY (Softly)

" In Thee, Lord ! do I put my trust, let me never be confounded."

(Then kneeling and laying her neck on the block... stretching out her arms with her Crucifix and Bible in each hand, and repeating many times)

MARY (Loudly)
" Into Thy hands, Lord! I commend my Spirit,"

(CURTAIN COMES DOWN)

(Three loud thuds... Her head is taken off with three strokes; The Dean crying out)

FLETCHER

"So let queen Elizabeth's enemies perish;"

The Earl of Kent answering...

KENT

'Amen'

MUSIC PLAYS..(EDITH PIAF...NO REGRETS)

**Non, Je Ne Regrette Rien (Lyrics) - Edith Piaf
https://youtu.be/IJvI0WNihyM via
@YouTube**

```
           THE END
```

Mary Queen of Scots...The Cross within my Loof.

My darkened bones lye in a cold, damp, dark n' dank Sarcophagus

For mony a year have been held captive in a foreign Acropolis

I went to death proud and true within my loof the Crucifix of Jesus for Him I died tho' not in vain

I was the queen o' bonnie France and Scotland was my hame!

Tho' mony a foe livin' there betrayed my short lived reign.

My faith from me they could nae take three times the axe upon my neck until my head did break.

Nae mair to me the Blackbird's song nae mair to me the tiny baby kitten,

Thru' lies conspiracy an' a Casket fu' o' forged letters written

My sister of England the queen she had been was false untrue her milk-less breasts were   smitten.

A parcel of rogues from the abyss of the

earth....

Cecil, Darnley, the bastard Morey n' Bothwell, John Knox n' barren Queen Elizabeth,
behold my name upon your breath an' face God for my death.

By Frank J Dougan

The word Loof is Old Scots for palm of hand.

Robert Burns... The Bard.....

Mony a year has passed since I took my last breath of Scottish air

Times have changed over 200 years gone my death was not fair

I wrote my works and believed in consequences rare
Now I see my dreams come true a Scotland with flair
Someday not far it will all come true the freedom of my bonnie land

Will draw a smile from me and a new sign from my hand
Mony people and friends will take up the understanding not bland

The beauty of the hills and lowlands my beautiful Scotland grand

United in peace no religion banned

Although I lay in a world of slumber my thoughts go out to you in years beyond

Never forget where your dreams are constantly in reality and the place of my birth is not a fatal house of gloom.

Now my name now welcome in Russia, Scotland, France , Australia and Canada afar

Loves young romance is in evidence in mony a twinkling star

My tragic beauty Mary Stuart to me is joined in the love we have in resplendence

Now together we are joined in the Kingdom of Our Lord we are

We live today in troubled times where haste is an expense.

Although I am long not here in this life my corps asleep the flesh rotten

The body of my works I wrote is still alive and not forgotten

Nae mair to me the summer sun will light upon my face

But mony a question is asked oe'r my grave Roman-cin'

Tho' I live within' the house of God my heart is dancin'.

By Frank J Dougan
1 January 2008

Lest we should forget Robert Burns and Mary Stuart

Robert Burns Dreams 2008......
A Jacobite I was born
The enforced Act of Union did I scorn
Revolution in the Americas and France

Disturbed the rich powerful intransigence
My ode's and poems a painful thorn
Within' the minds of the hated forgone
In Ayr and Dumfries I was a humble man
Mozart Beethoven Hayden

My brothers in art do understan'
Tho' now our music and words the world adorn.
We are all made from flesh and blood
As time goes by just turns to mud.

Man will come and man will go
Freedom, fraternity equality will win forever mo'
My love of Scotland the world does know

My devotion to God it is no show,
May the flowers of spring deck oe'r my grave gro'

By Frank J Dougan
24 January 2008

Dedicated to all you politicians who have forgotten the word FREEDOM

6th of April, 1320.
*' For as long as but one hundred of us remain alive,
we will never on any conditions submit to the domination of the English. It is not for glory nor riches, nor honours that we fight, but for freedom alone, which no good man gives up except with his life.'*

Part of The Declaration of Arbroath, written shortly after Robert De Brus had defeated English invaders at Bannockburn, following in the footsteps of Scotland's greatest warrior hero and defender of freedom William Wallace!

Oh Wallace William out of the west came to claim

justice, freedom and a nation for God his Lord's holy name, no cry or deed or want for himself of glory or fame.

At Stirling Bridge the might of Proud Edward's army fell,

the cream of England died, lived not a man to tell.

Victory for bold Wallace and his fighters,

river awash with invaders blood did swell.

The great General whom Napoleon followed his thought train,

half of one thousand years again.

A mountain of a man legendary robed in emerald green,

from the depth of the forests the Caledonian,

to free his beloved land from tyranny, wipe out oppression,

degradation, exploitation The Wallace cried 'Rebellion'.

From the mouth of the giant came!

' Dico tibi verum libertas optima rerum

nunquam servili sub nexu vivito fili'.

(Freedom is best I tell thee true, of all things to be won,

then never live within the bond of slavery my son!)

Reading, writing 'n speaking in tongues French, Gaelic, Latin,

this awesome intellectual warrior of history and science

The Celts to him they came with the crown of guardian.

Evil Edward now long forgotten of him no man will ken,

forever the indestructible name of the Wallace William

is revered in every glen.

Some day not far the nation of Scotland will sprout,

the cry goes out with thoughts of a Wallace shout

swords will be drawn battle lines take their form, every man stout,

Alba, Caledonia,
Scotland, the warrior hero William Wallace devout.

By Frank J. Dougan

Over 200 years had passed from the murder of Mary when the greatest Bard that ever lived

Robert Burns wrote of The Queen.

Taken from his Scots Prologue.....

Is there no daring bard will rise, and tell
How glorious Wallace stood and fell?
Where are the muses fled that could produce

A drama worthy o' the name o' Bruce;
How here, even here, he first unsheath'd the sword,
'Gainst mighty England and her guilty lord;

And after mony a bloody, deathless doing'
Wrench'd his dear country from the jaws of ruin?
O for a Shakespeare or an Otway scene,

To draw the lovely, hapless Scottish Queen!

*Vain all th' omnipotence of female charms
'Gainst headlong, Ruthless, Mad
rebellion's arms.*

*She fell, but fell with spirit Truly Roman,
To glut the vengeance of a rival woman:*

*A woman-tho' the phrase may seem uncivil-
As able and as cruel as the Devil!*

By Robert Burns

One can read the love and emotion that
Burns felt for Mary, as he himself was
living through the same trauma that she had
suffered in her dreams of freedom.
Robert Burns was oppressed most of his
adult life, as his writings were staunchly
Jacobean.

The Pitts of the English hierarchy used
every dirty trick in the book to discredit
the Bard because of his republican
rhetoric.

*Taken from the Lament of Mary Queen of
Scots.
By Robert Burns.....
-
I was the Queen o' bonnie France,
Where happy I hae been;
Fu' lightly rase I in the morn,*

As blythe lay down at e'en:
And I'm the sov'reign of Scotland,
And mony a Traitor there;
Yet here I lie in foreign bands,

And never-ending-care.

But as for thee, thou false woman!-

My sister and my fae,
Grim vengeance, yet, shall whet a sword
That thro' thy soul shall gae!

The weeping blood in woman's breast
Was never known to thee;
Nor the balm that draps on wounds of woe
Frae woman's pitying e'e.

My son! My son! May kinder stars
Upon thy fortune shine!

And may those pleasures gild thy reign,
That ne'er wad blink on mine!
God keep thee frae thy mother's faes,

Or turn their hearts to thee:
And where thou meet'st thy mother's friend,
Remember him for Me.

Oh! Soon, to me, may summer-suns
Nae mair light up the morn!

*Nae mair, to me, the autumn winds
Wave o'er the yellow corn!*

*And in the narrow house o' death
Let winter round me rave;*

And the next flow'rs, that deck the spring,

Bloom on my peaceful Grave.

　By Robert Burns

Milton Keynes UK
Ingram Content Group UK Ltd.
UKHW040638050923
428087UK00001B/52